A Life Less Punishing

13 Ways to Love the Life You've Got

MATT HEATH

The page numbers supplied with quotations are from the editions consulted by the author; refer to the 'References and Further Reading' section for more details.

First published in 2024

Allen & Unwin
Level 2, 10 College Hill, Freemans Bay
Auckland 1011, New Zealand
Phone: (64 9) 377 3800
Email: auckland@allenandunwin.com
Web: www.allenandunwin.co.nz

83 Alexander Street
Crows Nest NSW 2065, Australia
Phone: (61 2) 8425 0100

A catalogue record for this book is available from the National Library of New Zealand.

ISBN 978 1 99100 647 9

Design by Megan van Staden
Cover illustration by Renee Chin
Set in Baskerville 12/18
Printed and bound in Australia by the Opus Group

5 7 9 10 8 6

To my mum

Contents

Preface

> The mass of men lead lives of quiet desperation.
>
> —Henry David Thoreau, *Walden*, p. 8

It seems to me that no matter how good we have it, we modern humans make our short time on the planet more punishing than it needs to be. We spend years dissatisfied, worried, annoyed, scared, stressed, lonely, offended, angry or bored. Our go-to solutions to these problems — such as buying things we don't need, disappearing into technology and shoving as much as we can into our faces — don't seem to be working. So what can we do? Well, I believe we can read, listen and discuss our way out of most of the funks we get ourselves into. There's a lot to be said for searching out philosophies and scientific theories, trying them out on ourselves, working hard and finding out what helps. It's possible to make a hobby out of feeling better.

Emotions are often signals that we need to do something. Unfortunately, what we are supposed to do can be hard to work out. Luckily, our great species has been thinking about the condition of being us for many thousands of years. There are millions of suggestions on how we should live our lives. Some of them are terrible, fake and pointless; others might buy us a few moments of tranquillity here and there — but the best ones can help us become better, stronger humans, for ourselves, our friends, our families and everyone we run into.

I have a BA in Anthropology and Philosophy. So pretty much no qualification at all. Post-university I've spent my life in the entertainment industry. From *Back of the Y Masterpiece Television* (the TV show I made with my high-school buddies), to my band Deja Voodoo, to commentating sport with the Alternative Commentary Collective, to writing for the *New Zealand Herald*, to running an animation company with a friend and hosting *The Matt & Jerry Show* with another one, I've spent the past 25 years acting like an idiot on any medium that will have me. It's been great; but why, with such a dubious CV, do I think I have the right to write this book on life, philosophy and science?

The answer to this question begins with aliens on a school trip, the most powerful person on Earth, and a sad, intoxicated man sitting by a lake.

Introduction

The teacher, the emperor and the whingeing drunk

The 1980s TV show *The Greatest American Hero* followed the adventures of substitute teacher Ralph Hinkley and his encounter with extra-terrestrials on a class trip. The friendly aliens gifted him a superhero outfit packed with abilities. Unfortunately, Ralph loses the suit's instruction manual seconds after getting it and spends three frustrating years not knowing how to control his powers.

At the start of season three, a horrific global emergency brings the 'green guys' back to Earth with a new instruction manual for Ralph. When my three sisters and I saw the promos for the episode, we jumped up and down in front of the TV hugging and screaming in delight. At last, Mr Hinkley would be able to use the suit properly! No more losing control and flying into walls, or having his invisibility power fail at inopportune and embarrassing moments. Best of all, Ralph would have his powers just in time to defeat a cult of rabid Nazis. We couldn't have been more excited.

We were to be bitterly disappointed. Mr Hinkley got the manual, used it to shrink himself to the size of an ant — and then dropped it. He returned to normal, and never found the manual again. Ralph would blindly continue his chaotic adventures until the show was cancelled soon afterwards.

In the second century BCE, while on a military campaign in central Europe, Roman Emperor Marcus Aurelius kept a personal notebook on the correct way to behave in life. Marcus, the most powerful person on Earth, wasn't into orgies, torture or Colosseum-based slaughter like other leaders of the time. Instead, he focused his energies on virtue. He believed that his purpose was to serve humanity. When things went wrong, instead of feeding people to the lions, he chose to focus on his own failings. This journal, which was copied out by hand for many hundreds of years after his death, was written to himself, to remind him of the right things to do and to make sense of the terrible events that kept happening in his world. There were a lot. Marcus and his wife Faustina lost nine of their fourteen children, his best friend betrayed him and tried to take his throne, and half his empire died of smallpox. But the great man chose to transform frustrations into acceptance, anger into understanding, and challenges into opportunities. As he wrote:

> Does what's happened keep you from acting with justice, generosity, self-control, sanity, prudence, honesty, humility, straightforwardness, and all the other qualities that allow a person's nature to fulfill itself?
> —in *Meditations*, p. 48

In 2019, I am sitting on the shores of Lake Wakatipu feeling sorry for myself. The dark, cold water looks pretty good. Maybe I could just float away. My lovely mum died a few years before, and my sixteen-year relationship with the other best person I have ever met ended not long after that. Between those events and many failures, I've let a heavy sadness into my life. Adding to my troubles, I'm feeling ripped off by fitness. I'm down here with three of my friends for the Queenstown Marathon tomorrow (I am only running a half), and despite months of exercise aimed at feeling better, I'm still miserable. Even worse, this afternoon I heard 'Believe It or Not (theme from *The Greatest American Hero*)' by Joey Scarbury in a Queenstown chemist's. Great tune, but once it's in your brain you can't get it out.

Then, an epiphany. I stand up and triumphantly hiff my beer at a rubbish bin. I will combine Marcus Aurelius's journalling with Mr Hinkley's missing instructions. I will consume the writings, lectures and podcast appearances of great thinkers and regurgitate them into a personal Hinkley manual. It won't unlock superpowers, it won't be a work of genius, like *Meditations*, but it might stop me behaving like a tool every time a work-mate looks at me funny. When I'm feeling angry, stressed, worried or aimless in life, I'll look up those chapters and use them to calm the hell down. It will be a self-help book in its purest form, written for myself to help myself. That's a guaranteed A+, five stars, would-trade-again situation. My mission is now clear: I will read, listen and write my way out of the unshakeable sadness that has descended upon me, as it has on so many others in our little country.

* * *

Over the next few years, researching and implementing wellbeing strategies becomes an obsession. If I am running, I have a PDF reader or podcast blasting neuroscience or philosophy in my ears. I punish my friends, work-mates, family members, column readers and listeners constantly with the theories I have running through my head.

My father recently asked, 'Is there a single topic in this world that you haven't "recently" read a book on?' A better question from Dad would have been: 'Is there a book you've read that you can't shoehorn into a conversation on a different topic, just to show off that you have read it?'

The *New Zealand Herald* publishes my column once a week, but to call me a writer would be a stretch. I focus on crucial topics like 'Is my dog Colin the smartest in the world?', 'How to be a great hungover dad', and 'Can you tell if someone is good in bed by how well they parallel-park?' Over time, concepts from my personal wellbeing research leak into my articles. I start shoehorning in the brilliant theories of Gaius Musonius Rufus, Dr Anna Lembke, and my mate Spooge.

Eventually, my bosses take pity and give me the job of Happiness Editor. An honorary title that means little more than writing a second article each week focused on wellbeing. I jump at the opportunity and start using the paper's good name to tee up Zoom chats with my favourite thinkers from around the world.

But always in the back of my mind there is the sneaking suspicion that I have no right to be doing this and should shut up. The author of *The Grapes of Wrath*, John Steinbeck, once wrote in his journal: 'I am not a writer. I've been fooling myself and other people.' If *he* isn't a writer, what the hell am I? I have dangerously limited grammatical knowledge, and I recently humiliated myself on the TV show *Guy Montgomery's Guy Mont-Spelling Bee* by struggling to spell 'elephant' correctly.

I don't have survivor status. I've never had professional help for my sadness. I've never taken prescription drugs for it, and my drinking problem is close to functional. I have a fantastic family, and my two sons are exemplary human beings: loving, smart, caring, talented and fun to be around. Having them in my life should be enough to make anyone feel happy and proud every second of every day. I can't even take credit for that. My kids turning out great is down to luck, the amazing skills of their brilliant mother and the two episodes of *Supernanny* she made me watch before they were born.

On any sensible metric I have it good; there is no excuse for the sadness I experience. It's a disgrace. If I am unhappy, how the hell are people with real problems supposed to survive? How dare a man with so many blessings offer advice to people who are going through real problems?

One night, though, a guardian angel appears in my direct messages to bolster my confidence. This kind man's words of encouragement finally legitimised me as a writer. His message of hope — which, sadly, I delete more or less immediately — goes something like this:

> Fuck off with your middle class shit . . . you fucking loser. You're shit. Who the fuck do you think you are. I'm struggling with addiction. My wife won't let me see the kids. Seriously just shut up. Shuttttt up. No one wants to hear what you think. You're not tough. I could fuck you up.

While I have great sympathy for this poor man's plight, I immediately know he is wrong. Everyone has the right to share their thoughts and learnings with whomever they want. I'm not forcing people to read what I write. You can either believe it or not. It may not be relevant to you, but it might be to someone else. If you are doing it hard, I feel for you and I hope you can turn things around, but that doesn't make my thoughts worthless.

There are legions of the nearly alright who would like to feel happy for a larger proportion of the time they have left. We may hold it together on the outside but wake up at 3 a.m. riddled with crippling self-hatred, terrified about the future and desperately alone. We may not have meth addictions, we might be allowed to see our kids, and we may not feel the need to threaten people on Insta. But we *could* do with a few moments of peace here and there before we die. A little help confronting our raging negative emotions would be great.

Maybe my writing will help someone feel a little less desperate and disconnected; maybe it won't. Maybe something or someone else will. Either way, whoever you are, wherever you are — if you aren't feeling great, it's probably a good idea to do something about it.

* * *

Things went south quickly for the three buddies I was running with that day in Queenstown. While I was sitting up by the lake feeling sorry for myself, they were drawing closer to truly challenging and tragic times. Having pushed himself too hard, Joseph nearly died in hospital the next day; he was thrown in an ambulance with his finishing medal still round his neck.

G Lane finished the race with two very strange black eyes;

the following week he had some tests done and they discovered a rare type of cancer. A one-in-a-million thing. He spent the next two years having bone painfully removed from his forehead, unsure whether he would survive.

The way he dealt with this situation was one of the bravest things I have ever seen. Surgeons had to grind his skull off while he was awake, leaving a gruesome, painful hole in his head the size of a saucer. The final stage of his treatment involved the placement of large, fake-breast-like growths on his forehead to produce enough skin to cover the horrific cavity. It was truly grotesque. Through it all, with no guarantee he would survive, the man just kept going and going for his friends, work-mates and family. It was impressive to watch.

As for my good mate Scotty, less than a year after the race his lovely wife and the mother of their two beautiful sons was diagnosed with a brain tumour. She died a year after that. Tragic beyond words.

So. The only person in our group with no major problems on the horizon is the one sulking by the lake — me. A sad little man not yet capable of gratitude for the life he has.

As I was writing this, American hip hop artist and actor Ice-T posted this on Instagram:

> When you ARE having real fun and are Truly Happy.
> ENJOY it to the fullest! Cause Pain is inevitably coming.

He is right of course. Bad stuff is on the way for all of us — such is the nature of the universe. Best we appreciate what we have at this moment, because it might not get any better.

* * *

When I told a close friend who runs a messy house that I was writing this book, she laughed. 'But you're crazy, that's like me writing a book on cleaning.' Another friend put it this way: 'You don't know shit and you can't spell.' Both fair criticisms.

Some of this book won't make sense to you. Some of it might not make sense to anyone. The same concepts will be repeated, many of which you will have seen elsewhere. You will probably roll your eyes at how obvious some of it is. (Last week, I saw one of the quotes I use in this book scrawled on the wall of the London Underground.)

I suffer from aggressive adaptive memory distortion, powerful Dunning–Kruger (a form of bias in which someone lacking knowledge and skills in a particular area overestimates their competence in that very area) and, at the time of writing, a terrible hangover. There will be misrepresentations and misunderstandings of both great and poor ideas. The logical fallacy of appealing to authority is a problem, especially when it comes to my boy Marcus. But a few years ago, Tim Clare (the British author of an exceptionally helpful and deep book titled *Coward: Why we get anxious & what we can do about it*) gave me the following advice:

> If you have a favourite kind of pie, I can't go up to you and say: I just did a study, and two-thirds of people like something else, so your favourite is wrong. If it is your favourite, no one can take that away. It's the same with anything to do with mental health. If it helped you, you've done some kind of study on yourself. It's a one equals one, and you feel better. It's kind of the end of the argument for you personally. Even if across a lot of people in a study, it might not pan out.

If this is the case — and it might not be, it seems pretty anecdotal — but if it is, then this is a book full of my pies. A rendering-down of theories that convinced me of their worth over thousands of hours of listening, reading and punishing my friends with my chat over coffees and beers.

Each chapter will begin (mostly) with a humiliating story from my life, followed by an exploration of the philosophy, history and science I have since discovered that I believe helped me. Some of these personal stories are so embarrassing that if you see me on the street you'll cross the road in disgust — and those are just the ones I actually own up to. In the really horrific stories I'll change my name to protect my identity.

Important philosophies, studies and theories will be missed because I didn't read them or they didn't tickle my fancy. This is in no way a complete look into any of the issues raised. It is simply a detailed regurgitation of some of the things that helped me quell my anger, thicken my skin and lower my terror levels. Ideas that I believe enabled me to become a better father, friend, family member, work-mate, member of society, and human. Concepts that eased my feelings of loss, got me off my devices, stopped me worrying about death 24/7, lost me 12 kilograms and helped me sleep slightly better at night. If you have serious issues, you should reach out for real professional help. This book is not that.

Some people say that we should picture our dreams and the universe will provide. That's rubbish. Wishing won't change anything and the universe is more likely to throw challenges your way than to help. If there are things you want to achieve you have to do the work. We can, however, make it easier for ourselves by learning to handle whatever comes our way. To take charge of our own minds, accept what happens in the real world and base our responses on that. If we concentrate our energies on doing honourable things with the stuff under our remit, we might find a sniff of meaning before we die.

It is often said that youth is wasted on the young, but the middle-aged and elderly are more than capable of squandering the time they have. It doesn't matter how many precious years, minutes or seconds we get on the planet, we can all find ways not to appreciate what we have. Instead, we could choose to calm the hell down and find some gratitude, contentment and tranquillity. I've been doing those very things a lot over the past few years, and I have to say that my life is much less punishing than it used to be.

This book celebrates the heights of virtue, reason, love and self-control. But there is no judgement here. These are targets few, if any, humans reach. I, for one, regularly catch myself scoring own-goals, whingeing and behaving terribly. Nonetheless, it is nice to have ideals to aspire to. As neurosurgeon and terminal cancer patient Paul Kalanithi wrote:

> You can't ever reach perfection, but you can believe in an asymptote toward which you are ceaselessly striving. —in *When Breath Becomes Air*, p. 146

This is my attempt at Ralph Hinkley's instruction manual mixed with Marcus's journal. It's nowhere near as good as either. Enjoy.

Love,
Matt Heath

Chapter One

Angry?

> Some . . . have called anger a short madness: for it is equally devoid of self control, regardless of decorum, forgetful of kinship, obstinately engrossed in whatever it begins to do, deaf to reason and advice . . .
> —Lucius Annaeus Seneca, *On Anger*, p. 3.

When I was a kid, Tim Finn from the Kiwi rock band Split Enz was my hero. I listened to his music and talked about the man so much that my lovely mother made me a Tim Finn soft toy for my eighth birthday. Years later when I finally met him, a stupid violent rage messed everything up, including his dressing room.

It's 2003, and shared management has my band Deja Voodoo on tour in support of Tim. Thanks to our stunt-based TV show *Back of the Y*, we are booked to play songs and then, just before the headline act, smash burning guitars over bass player Chris's head. The second night into the tour, I swing a guitar lower than planned and break two of his ribs. Chris is a tough individual. He not only stars in our TV show, but also directs it and serves as the chief stuntman. He never flinches or complains, even in the most challenging situations. But a friend behaving this recklessly with your personal safety would aggravate anyone.

At soundcheck the following day, I suggest we practise a song we have been struggling with to make sure we get it right. Chris suggests we don't. Unfortunately he delivers his suggestion in a sarcastic and aggressive tone. By this time the guy has been cutting me off, putting down my ideas, insulting me and belittling me for days. I feel hurt. It's eating me up inside. So I escalate the situation by demanding we practise the whole song *five times*. Chris tells me to shut up; I tell him to piss off. He looks around at the band and crew with a smirk and yells, in a baby voice: 'Matt's going to throw a tanty.' So I drop my guitar and hold my middle finger right up to his face. Insanity and wrath take over. Before you know it, we are deep in an on-stage fist-fight. The scrap spills down the stairs, through a hallway and into my childhood idol's private dressing room. My whole life I dreamed of meeting Tim Finn. Today I scare the crap out of him with an uninvited brawl.

Tim backs up against the wall to protect himself as I'm pushed through a table of pre-show canapés. Somehow I grab one of Chris's shoes and use it to beat him around the head. Tim politely asks, 'Is this a gag? Is this for your TV show?' But we are too far gone to answer. The sweaty, screaming fight continues, until anger eventually subsides. I'm left on the floor, red-faced, sore and embarrassed. What the hell happened? Was I possessed by demons? Chris was right — I did throw a tanty.

In a testament to what a good guy he is, and likely also to all the crazy stuff he has seen in the business, Tim doesn't kick us off the tour, but my dreams of my idol becoming my best friend have been destroyed along with the glasses on his dressing-room table.

When I asked Tim about the incident recently, he said with a smile: 'You guys were intense.'

* * *

Anger is part of our instinct to fight off threats, to compete for resources and to enforce social norms. In the old world, when a snake jumped out of the undergrowth and attacked us the primitive parts of our brains fired up and flooded our systems with stress hormones like cortisol, adrenaline and testosterone, which motivate powerful physical action. Without anger, our ancestors wouldn't have lasted long. A slow response wasn't an option.

The amygdala is a small almond-shaped part of our brain that scientists believe senses danger, triggers anger and motivates action. It's sometimes referred to as the lizard brain — an ancient part of our mind that has been with us since we parted ways with reptiles and all the way back to when we were fish. The lizard brain is in charge of our 'fight, flight, feeding, freezing up, and fornication', as Dr Joseph Troncale puts it on the Psychology Today website.

Meanwhile, the prefrontal cortex is the area that exerts control over our actions, through employing reason and judgement when alerted to danger. One part fires us up automatically, and the other attempts to control that response. Of course anger isn't always a reaction to real events; there's also a purely psychological side. We can become angry at things we have made up. We are quite capable of imagining ourselves into rage.

Anger causes all kinds of problems for modern folk. Screaming, punching and flailing around might help us deal with a snake attack, but it's unlikely to solve modern domestic, transport or employment issues. Unfortunately, our amygdala is unaware that things have changed. It has no idea that we live in a relatively safe modern environment. To this primal part of the brain, an air-conditioned office in central Auckland is the same as the savanna one million years ago. We can enter fight mode over a social-media post, an IT-enforced password change, a botched hotel booking, or how many times to rehearse a song.

Whereas emotions like fear (also associated with the amygdala) might motivate us to leave a situation, anger can cause us to move towards danger and create more problems when we get there. Once you're in, it's hard to get back out — you get carried along with the rage of it all. Left unchecked, anger can cause untold damage to you, your family, friends, society — maybe even the world.

> No plague has cost the human race more. We see all around us people being killed, poisoned, and sued; we see cities and nations ruined. And besides destroying cities and nations, anger can destroy us individually.
> —Lucius Annaeus Seneca, *On Anger*, p. 11

So what can we do? The first step in our battle against anger is to acknowledge that it's (usually) a bad thing. If we accept that it doesn't achieve our goals and instead interferes with our problem-solving, we'll start to push back. If we believe it's okay or helpful — as I did for most of my life — we are unlikely to put in the effort to control it. That's why it's a good idea to take a look at your anger. Viewed from the outside, the childishness, popping veins and flying saliva of rage does not look cool. Observe your angry behaviour, and you will likely find it embarrassing and look for a better option.

I've seen footage of myself mid-rage and it was not good. I got very red in the face. Veins popped, my nose screwed up, terrible things were said to a co-host on *The Matt & Jerry Show*. This particular incident captured on video inflicted considerable damage to my reputation, my self-respect and my new HD monitor.

> How much more damage anger does than the things that cause it. —Marcus Aurelius, *Meditations*, p. 153

The worlds of celebrity, history and news provide us with plenty of examples of damaging rage that we can observe, laugh at and learn from. Take the brilliant actor Russell Crowe, who was arrested and cuffed in 2005 after hitting a Soho hotel receptionist in the face with a phone he threw because he couldn't get through to his wife. Not a great move — a long way from the 'strength and honour' you might expect from the man who played the great Maximus in *Gladiator*. And how about French football legend Zinedine Zidane, sent off in the last match of his career after head-butting Italian player Marco Materazzi in the 2006 World Cup final? A moment of madness that overshadowed a lot of what he'd achieved to that point; not the way he wanted to end things.

Then there's Will Smith losing his rag at a joke and slapping Chris Rock on stage at the 2022 Academy Awards. How much worse were the consequences of the Fresh Prince's anger compared to the cause of it? Up until that moment he was the good guy of Hollywood, enjoying near-universal admiration and on the cusp of the greatest moment of his career — a deserved Best Actor Oscar for *King Richard*. Then he lets wrath take over, jumps up from his special very important person chair, and delivers a whack across the face of a much smaller man, before slumping back down to yell some humiliating 'tough guy' abuse. A few moments of craziness, and that's it for his reputation. The debacle results in multiple project cancellations, erases the hard work of everyone else on the film, and pushes

Smith's personal life into further disarray. Meanwhile, Chris Rock's calm response enhanced his reputation and created new opportunities — earning him a rumoured 40 million in Netflix dollars for his next special.

History is also packed with cautionary tales. Co-emperor Valentinian ruled the western half of the Roman Empire from 364 CE until he yelled himself to death in a fit of anger on his fifty-fourth birthday. He'd been battling the Quadi tribe for years with limited success. One day an ambitious diplomat came up with a cunning plan to end the conflict. He invited the leaders of the Quadi to a peace banquet. Picture the scene: the food is delicious, the wine exceptional and the entertainment top-notch. Everyone is having a great time until a bunch of Roman soldiers jump out and slit every single Quadi's throat from ear to ear.

Non-attending Quadi were understandably furious at this turn of events and spent the next few years running amok in Roman territory. Valentinian eventually quelled the Quadi enough that they were willing to talk again, and another peace meeting was organised. It didn't go well.

Valentinian believed that he had God-like authority to rule, and his word was truth no matter what happened. So he turned up to the meeting expecting bended knees, gifts and grovelling apologies from the Quadi. Instead, the representatives of the Quadi pointed out that the Romans started the whole conflict by building forts in Quadi lands and killing everyone at the last peace banquet. This is of course true and everyone knows it.

But that doesn't stop the Roman co-emperor from completely losing it. There are many descriptions of what happened next, but I like this one by blogger JW:

> [Valentinian] started screaming. And yelling. And screaming some more. He was hysterical. He was apoplectic.
>
> He was also very shortly quite dead.
>
> The human body [doesn't] deal especially well with long periods of great stress, which this encounter would certainly count as for our dear emperor. As Valentinian was in the middle of berating the Quadi, he suddenly fell over and unceremoniously collapsed to the floor where he died of a brain hemorrhage.

Then there are the everyday angry people.

In February 2023, 50-year-old Georgia woman Belinda Miller discovers that the biscuits are missing from her fast-food order. Staffers have already admitted their mistake and supplied her with the absent snacks, but this isn't enough for Belinda. She becomes enraged and plots violent revenge. According to a Richmond County Sheriff's Office incident report, she returned and crashed into the entrance of the restaurant in her SUV, just missing an 18-year-old employee.

Looking in from the outside, it seems clear that throwing phones, slapping comedians and ram-raiding fast-food restaurants won't solve our problems. In each of these cases, anger creates more difficulties than it solves. Prisons are full of people who have gotten angry and made things worse.

Further down the scale, an angry knee-jerk text might start a two-day argument with someone you love; losing your cool in a meeting could lose you business; screaming at your children may push them away from you; and giving the bird to another motorist might earn you a tyre-iron around the back of your head. Anger can pollute, sour and destroy the best years of your life. That's why it might be worth observing your own anger and calling to mind Our Russ, Will Smith and Belinda Miller of Georgia next time you feel yourself heating up.

But what about those times when anger *is* justified?

THE CASE FOR ANGER

While anger can clearly do terrible damage, sometimes in life we see wrongs being committed; wrongs that seem to deserve a powerful, passionate response. You don't want to spend your life enraged — but surely it's okay to fire up every now and then for the right cause? The Bible thinks so.

Righteous rage: In the fourth century, a monk named Evagrius Ponticus listed 'eight evil thoughts': gluttony, lust, avarice, sloth, sadness, vainglory, pride and anger. These were later cut back to seven, and anger become wrath; likely because Christianity has a place for righteous anger but not uncontrollable rage. Take Jesus — by all accounts a mellow guy, but even he lost his temper from time to time.

> And Jesus went into the temple of God, and cast out all them that sold and bought in the temple, and overthrew the tables of the money changers, and the seats of them that sold doves, And said unto them, It is written, My house shall be called the house of prayer; but ye have made it a den of thieves. —*Holy Bible: King James Version*, Matthew 21:12–13

On the whole, the Bible is supportive of anger fuelled by righteousness. Jesus' behaviour at the temple is okay because it is considered to be justifiable. Similarly, the God of the First Testament gets really angry and often, but it is always directed at sin. Something he really dislikes.

> And the anger of the LORD was kindled against Uzzah; and God smote him there for his error; and there he died by the ark of God. —*Holy Bible: King James Version*, 2 Samuel 6:6–7

The ancient Greek philosopher Aristotle was also a fan of righteous anger.

> The man who is angry at the right things and with the right people, and, further, as he ought, when he ought, and as long as he ought, is praised. This will be the good-tempered man, then, since good temper is praised. —in *Aristotle: The complete works*, p. 996

We all have moments in our life when it feels like a bit of passion is needed. Anger can cut through where a 'quiet word' cannot. You could call these outbursts stern chats, righteous indignation or a serious talking-to.

Where I come from, the act of angrily yelling at someone is referred to as a 'southerly', after the bone-chilling wind that plagues the lower South Island. In the 1990s my dad delivered me a well-deserved and life-changing southerly. I was putting my new car through its paces on a windy road near our farm. He was coming home the other way. During an attempted hand-brake turn around a tight bend, I ran Dad off the road. Seeing what I had done and knowing how much trouble I was in, I sped off, screamed up our driveway, sprinted across a field, dived into the barn and bolted the doors.

A righteous wrath would soon descend upon me. Dad, the calmest, most softly spoken man you could ever hope to meet, banged on the barn door so hard and passionately I thought it would break. He informed me — more loudly than I had ever heard anyone yell before — that 'I was a stupid little boy', adding, 'JESUS FUCKING CHRIST, Matthew, are you insane?

You will kill someone driving like that.' The message cut right through the door, through the hay bales I was hiding behind, and into my soul. Dad's anger was logical, helpful and backed by a scary passion. There was rage there, but I deserved it. It was a powerful righteous southerly.

I hid in there until it was dark and everyone was asleep. Luckily, my kind mum had put my dinner in the microwave so I could sneak in and heat it up.

Anger as a strategy: The second test in the 1986 All Blacks' tour of France, played at Stade de la Beaujoire, is known to this day as the 'Battle of Nantes'. The French played with furious rage. Things were so intense that twenty minutes into the game, captain-to-be Wayne 'Buck' Shelford came out of an aggressive ruck with three teeth missing and his scrotum ripped open, leaving a testicle hanging free. The French scored a rare victory over the All Blacks, 16–3. From the outside it seemed like they were using anger to their advantage. So can rage create some kind of singular focus that gives you the edge? It seems likely that anger evolved, in part at least, to get the hormones flowing that we need for direct action.

There's been some speculation over the years that the rage of the French that day was fuelled by amphetamines . . . If so, it wouldn't be the first time that drugs have been used to fire combatants up for battle.

According to legend, berserkers were Norse fighters who

attacked enemies in a trance-like fury. It's from them we get our word 'berserk'. They ran fearlessly into battle, often nude and high on magic mushrooms. Tales of their fierceness spread, making the enemy more likely to run away in fear. However, there are questions about the statistical utility of a berserker over multiple battles. Sometimes they would become confused, veer off course and attack innocent trees. On really bad days they would get so disorientated that they'd circle right around and wreak havoc on their own side. You can imagine a Viking commander slapping his forehead in frustration as his nude, wasted berserkers hack up members of his own invading force. Rage is chaotic and brings no guarantees. Over time, a calmer strategical approach may generate more consistent results.

Whether it works as a battle strategy or not, one thing seems likely: full mushroom-induced nude rage wouldn't have been a solid long-term career option for the berserkers themselves. Those first off the boat, no matter their anger level, are likely to get an arrow through the head.

* * *

American clinical psychologist and global performance coach Dr Michelle Cleere believes that anger has limited value in sport because athletes struggle to refocus. They are often unable to move past the event that aggravated them, making it hard to concentrate on their performance. Not only that, but it increases muscle tension, heart rate and breathing rate unnecessarily.

She thinks that anger takes energy away from where it needs to be in your muscles and mind. This tends to have a lasting negative effect over the course of a longer competition. So you might get lucky and win a game or damage the opposition's downstairs, but anger isn't a great season-long strategy.

Over a beer in 2023, I asked former All Blacks captain Kieran 'Eye Sockets' Read for his thoughts on anger across his 125 international caps. He told me:

> I don't buy that to be aggressive you need to be angry, so I never felt the need to look for something to make me that way. In fact, if I got angry on the field it tended to be to the detriment of my game because it basically stopped me from making great decisions, etc. As a captain, there would be times where an angry response was needed to be given to the team to snap them out of a funk, however you always need to coincide the message with solutions and a way forward. As a captain I would use yelling and ranting as a tool to motivate the forwards around me, but I wasn't really angry (as I'm not that person).

While wasted berserkers and rucking Frenchmen probably go too far down the rage route, most people would say that a passionate, angry rebuke coming from a good place is okay; that allowing yourself to be taken over by rage has utility. But not the Stoics . . .

REJECTING ANGER

The Stoics were a group of philosophers who emerged in Ancient Greece around the third century BCE. They followed Stoicism, a philosophy founded by Zeno of Citium, which teaches the development of self-control and virtue as a means of overcoming destructive emotions. These Stoics believed that understanding the natural order of the world was the best way to align ourselves with it and help us lead a virtuous life of wisdom, courage, justice and temperance.

Stoicism spread to Rome, where businessman, dramatist and Stoic philosopher Lucius Annaeus Seneca (4 BCE–65 CE) became one of its most famous proponents. He knew a bit about controlling anger. Seneca worked for the debauched, sadistic and infuriating emperor Nero — a man who allegedly murdered his own mother, beat his pregnant wife to death (so he could marry a man who looked like her), and according to some accounts had Christians set on fire like candles, to illuminate his gardens.

Eventually the paranoid emperor turned on Seneca, as he had everyone else in his life. He decided that the great philosopher was plotting against him and ordered Seneca's death — demanding that his long-time adviser perform this on himself. Seneca had every right to scream and yell and rage against this unjust turn of events; but instead, his calm, virtuous response has echoed through the ages. His death is the subject of dozens of iconic paintings of which Peter Paul Rubens' 1615 work *The Death of Seneca* is the most well known. It's a powerful representation of strength and honour. I have a print of it in the downstairs bathroom; it keeps me honest in the mornings.

When the big day came, Seneca slashed his veins without complaint, but bled too slowly so politely asked for some hemlock. When that didn't kill him, he calmly requested those enforcing his death to run a hot bath to speed up the toxins. His wife, Pompeia Paulina, understandably upset, attempted to take her own life, too, but Seneca embraced her and asked her not to grieve too much.

Seneca saw no point in being angry about a death sentence he couldn't alter. Screaming and struggling and ranting wouldn't change the outcome — he would die no matter what, so he chose to stay calm, keep his dignity and make the process as pleasant as he could for his friends, his family and even his executioners.

Seneca believed that no matter what happens, we should maintain a rational state of mind. Focus on what we can control while accepting what we cannot. Respond to reality with reason. We have power over how we feel internally and how we react to events. In his opinion, no matter the circumstances we should choose not to be angry, because anger doesn't help us reach our goals. He believed that it pushes us towards confrontation, danger and retaliation and never makes things better.

Seneca's death sets a high bar in terms of keeping your cool in an aggravating situation. Few of us could pull *that* off. We can, however, use Seneca as inspiration to keep calm and act logically in our day-to-day lives. If Seneca could behave with dignity when forced to slit his own wrists for a crime he hadn't committed, what excuse do we have for anger about trivial things in our lives? We allow ourselves to become furious over traffic, stubbed toes, snarky comments or opposing political opinions. But if we call to mind the calmness with which Seneca faced his death, we might respond to the mislaying of our car keys without yelling at our loved ones.

MANAGING ANGER

> The best plan is to reject straightway the first incentives to anger, to resist its very beginnings, and to take care not to be betrayed into it: for if once it begins to carry us away, it is hard to get back again into a healthy condition. —Lucius Annaeus Seneca, *On Anger*, p. 18

Seneca advises destroying anger the moment it arises. Don't give it an inch. Shut it down the second that its impulses fire up from the more primitive parts of our brains. At this point, he believed, we have a choice: ride our brain's crazy suggestions to destruction, or jump off.

If you want to move on from anger you'll have to employ your prefrontal cortex, the area of the brain that involves itself in reasoning and decision-making. The PFC is able to look forward, simulate outcomes and see a fuller picture. Unfortunately, the amygdala and other ancient instinctual parts of the brain are faster — they rev you up immediately. The reasoning part of the brain takes a while to formulate a counter-argument.

Often, by the time your decision-making brain kicks in, you've already done the crazy thing. Kicked the flat tyre and broken your foot, insulted your sisters, or thrown your friend through a table of snacks in your hero's dressing room.

We like to believe that the conscious, reasoning part of our mind is predominantly in charge of our decisions. However, our conscious mind is actually a wuss that gets bossed, harassed and bullied by our subconscious. Luckily, there is a simple way we can buy time for our rational side to take over. One that parents have been pushing for generations.

Like many little boys, I was a hot-head. If I fired up, my lovely mum would say: 'Matthew, look at me . . . Now take a few breaths, okay, and count to ten — don't think about anything, just count and then we can talk about it.' Moments later I would be hard-pressed to remember what had aggravated me.

Kiwi counsellor and mindfulness coach Rebekah Ballagh (author of *Big Feelings: And what they tell us*) told me on a Zoom call that this simple method works for kids and adults alike.

> Anger is a sign that you are dysregulated at any age. It's a threat response. If anger has led you to flip your lid, you're not seeing things clearly. So it's useful to use any tool that will help bring you back to being a little bit more logical. So things like deep breathing activate our parasympathetic nervous system.

As simplistic, clichéd and obvious as it seems, counting in your mind, taking a few breaths and choosing to delay your response *works*. It gives your PFC the time it needs to jump in. Often, when our logical thinking takes over, we discover that our anger response was wrongly triggered.

> We ought not to fly into a rage even when the injury appears to be open and distinct: for some false things bear the semblance of truth. We should always allow some time to elapse, for time discloses the truth.
>
> —Lucius Annaeus Seneca, *On Anger*, p. 55

My dog, Colin, was attacked by an off-leash whippet a couple of years ago. My immediate instinct was to punch both the owner and the dog in the head. (That would have been a mistake — the man involved was ex South African Special Forces; he could have killed me.) Instead I took a few breaths and let things calm down. As it turns out, he felt bad, helped with Colin and we are now friends. Faff is a good man to have on my side. He has a lovely wife, too. They both helped me with a branch that fell down in my yard a few weeks back. Really glad now I didn't assault him or Tiger; I would have struggled to forgive myself if I had punched that beautiful whippet in the face. For his part, Colin forgave everyone involved two seconds after the attack.

So, whether you're five or 65, the advice around anger from neuroscientists, Seneca and my mum is the same. Take a few deep breaths, maybe count to ten. Create time to formulate a sensible response.

* * *

Once we have bought ourselves some space, we can employ strategies to help us move on and deliver an advantageous response.

Our human brains are powerful, and can interrupt events in our lives in a number of ways. Philosophy professor William B. Irvine described an incident to me via Zoom in April 2022. You are running in a park and someone tackles you to the ground from behind. You hit the turf hard. It hurts. Surely you have every right to be angry at the person who has attacked you? But then Irvine adds some more information. At the time you are knocked to the ground you are playing American football, and the tackle is legal under the rules of the game. The attack has the exact same physical result. You hit the ground just as hard. You feel the same pain. The only difference is your framing of the event. It's a game, so it's fine.

A bad hangover is challenging, but we know why it's here and that it will go away. Those exact same symptoms might be terrifying if they appeared out of the blue or were part of an ongoing illness.

Our perspective determines whether we see an event as positive, negative or neutral. Are you missing out on a party, or resting up to enjoy your day tomorrow? Stuck in traffic, or gifted time to listen to a podcast? Involved in a boring house shift, or getting a workout? Your life gets a lot easier if you choose to interpret things in a positive way. Irvine took me through a few of his most successful reframing techniques.

Hanlon's razor: This is a handy rule of thumb that goes: 'Never attribute to malice that which is adequately explained by stupidity.'

Suppose a hotel clerk loses your reservation. Yes, he *might* have done so on purpose, but more likely he is simply incompetent. Frame the incident as incompetence rather than malice, and the emotion you subsequently experience may well be pity rather than anger.

Story mode: In the midst of frustrating events, you might want to flip your perspective to story mode. All decent tales have a protagonist (a good guy) and an antagonist (a bad guy). Instead of getting angry, concentrate on the story that's being created around you and try to be the good guy. The more complex things get, the better the yarn you will have to share with friends later.

As a broadcaster I need stories to fill my radio shows, articles, TV appearances and podcasts. We call this content 'casual chats'. Run out of gas in the middle of a busy road and end up in the back of a police car — casual chat. Cat jumps up and eats the burger out of your hand — casual chat. Heart-breaking dumping by your girlfriend — casual chat.

Recently I was hit by a car while riding my bike to work, and as I slid across the intersection I thought to myself 'Casual chat'. That potentially aggravating crash has since been the subject of three articles, two radio shows, a podcast and now it's here. I sent the driver a bottle of whisky to thank him for the content.

Finitude: The ultimate perspective-changer is, of course, death. Sam Harris (the neuroscientist) asks if anger makes any sense considering the imminent tragedy we all face. He discusses the absurdity of road rage, suggesting that instead of firing up, you could attempt to find some empathy. You can do this by bringing to mind the fact that both you and the person who's aggravating you on the road are going to die one day. That sooner or later both of you will lose everyone you love. You could also focus on the happy fact that you are alive and able to drive, and not sick and dying in a hospital bed. That your children or others you love are alive. That you're not living in a country where people are being rounded up and murdered for who they are or what they believe in. If you concentrate on those things, it's hard to stay angry.

You could remind yourself that, whatever moment you are in now, you will never get it back and you don't know how many more moments you will have. Everything you do in life, from breathing, to driving, to communicating with those you love, you will one day do for the last time. We don't have long here. Do you want to spend the precious moments you have left red-faced, screaming and waving your middle finger at a stranger? With a shortness-of-life perspective, anger is difficult to maintain. More on this in the chapter on grieving.

PEACE, LOVE . . . AND GOLF

Everywhere we go on this chaotic planet we will find opportunities to pit ourselves against our rage.

My fifteen-year-old son and I have arrived at a local golf course for a quick nine. He's looking forward to smashing me by at least ten shots, but there's a problem — a group of older gentlemen ahead of us are taking ages to tee off.

All good. It's a sunny day, and I chat with my boy about life for a few minutes. We can wait. This is not good enough for one of the older men, though. He marches over and snarls, 'Are you allowed to be here?'

I respond: 'Happy new year, sir. Yes, we are.'

And he replies, 'You can't play if you haven't paid. They have video, they will catch you.'

How goddamn rude of this man. How dare he assume we aren't supposed to be here simply from the way we look.

The old me — the one that beat his friend with a shoe in Tim Finn's dressing room — would have lost it at this point. I would have done or said something to escalate the situation. Instead, I take a breath, buy time for reason to kick in, and reframe the situation. I choose empathy. I don't know what pain this old man has experienced or is currently dealing with; at his age, he will have lost loved ones. He may not have long left on this Earth. My anger devolves into pity.

I smile at the man, put my arm around my son's shoulder and answer calmly: 'We are legit, chief; I assume you are, too. Looking forward to teeing off as soon as you fellas get going.'

The old man responds, 'We are members of the club, you know?' This guy really wants a confrontation. So I call to mind some words of Marcus Aurelius from *Meditations* (p. 69), 'The best revenge is not to be like that', and I reply: 'Good for you, and what a lovely course it is.'

My friendliness is overwhelming. He has no choice but to retreat, defeated in the face of my toothy smile. Deep down in his soul, this angry man is likely aware that he's in the wrong. I look at my son; he's relieved the situation was defused. He's seen me get angry at people before, and prefers this version of Dad.

I feel pride in the way I behaved. Someone wanted to belittle me, but instead gifted me the opportunity to demonstrate calmness and virtue in front of my son. I have made great strides in the battle against that demon anger.

Moments later, I spray my drive miles to the right, sending the ball smashing into a building development next door. I scream in anger and attempt to break my club over my leg. The breathing comes too late this time; I am a work in progress.

This behaviour also pleases my son.

Chapter Two

Dissatisfied?

Cologne, September 2007: an inner-city theatre is crammed with German movie fans. They are here to see *The Devil Dared Me To*, a feature film starring my buddy, myself and a bunch of other people who (unlike us) can actually act. *Devil* is a filthy comedy flick that tracks the fictional rise of stuntman Randy Cambell from a rural loser with a lust for danger to a national superstar who wants to kill himself. As the promo blurb reads:

> Every kiwi lad dreams of greatness. But for little Randy Cambell, the dream is as big as the stunts his not-so-death-defying father died attempting. Young Randy Cambell yearns to be NZ's greatest living stuntman, much to the chagrin of his aunt and uncle who understand that the petrol running in Randy's veins is bound to ignite one day.

Globally, the movie has sold pretty well; it's made its budget back and — in a rare event for New Zealand cinema — the cast and crew have been paid out on their profit points. Things are going well for *The Devil Dared Me To* . . . Or are they?

The lights go down and the movie opens with a beautiful shot of New Zealand from space, before zooming down to a desolate South Island hilltop. A cute little eight-year-old, Randy, smokes a cig before attempting to jump 22 kilometres across Cook Strait on a kid's bike. He makes it about one metre before smashing to the ground and badly injuring himself. The crowd explodes in laughter as the little boy cries.

Then it all goes horribly wrong. The words 'What a load of shit' echo out across the theatre. Two drunk losers at the back are ruining the screening for everyone. They boo and heckle the movie. 'This is crap!' screams one. The other one yells, 'Boring!' The first one adds, 'German beer is really strong . . .' After a few minutes, the abusive duo are asked to leave. This is a problem, as these haters are the director, producer, stars and writers of the film. These two absolute punishers are me and Chris Stapp (aka Randy). We shot *Devil* back home two years earlier and are now on tour promoting it at film festivals across the globe. Each night we introduce the film and run a Q&A session afterwards.

You'd think the creators of a feature film would love travelling the world, staying in five-star hotels and being wined, dined, admired and chauffeured. Surely they would be grateful that the culmination of three years of hard work is receiving some recognition? But nah. We booed our movie in Hamburg and in Berlin, too, and I walked out on it in London and Timaru.

Two days after the Cologne screening I find myself sitting on a beach in Spain reading *The Stranger* by Albert Camus, a deeply depressing French novel from 1942 on the meaninglessness of human life. I look over at Chris; he's hunched over a sketch pad drawing the Grim Reaper.

If you feel dissatisfied on an all-expenses paid, pampered, luxury tour of the world celebrating a movie you star in, then you will find dissatisfaction wherever you go.

SO WHAT'S HAPPENING HERE?

One of the big questions of our time is this: why do the richest countries, like ours, who have it the best, suffer the most anxiety, depression and suicide? As American psychiatrist and author of *Dopamine Nation* Dr Anna Lembke puts it:

> [We have] lots of food, lots of fun stuff, lots of medicines to protect us from illness and pain, [but] we've clearly reached some kind of tipping point; we're now essentially more miserable than ever. —in YouTube video on dopamine fasting

She believes it has a lot to do with the co-location of our pleasure and pain processing centres. A part of our brain called the ventral pallidum works like a reward seesaw, with pleasure on one side and pain on the other. It doesn't like to be tipped either way for long. So when we experience pleasure, it piles pain onto the other side to even things out. This push for balance (called homeostasis) is true across most of our biology — when we get too hot, we sweat to cool down; when we get too cold, we shiver to heat up.

Lembke talks about little 'gremlins' that represent neuroadaptation. If we eat a packet of chips, the seesaw tips over to the pleasure side. To balance this out, the gremlins jump on to the pain side and stay there until things tip back the other way. This is how pleasure leads to pain — you get an equal amount of pain to balance out the pleasure. We might call it a comedown. That's the moment you want more chips, booze, or whatever pleasure-inducing thing you were doing. Now, you're wanting pleasure to move things back away from the pain. This is a big problem for those of us living in the richest countries in the world, because our modern lives are so packed with pleasant substances, experiences and behaviours that our reward pathways have become stressed. All that pleasure is making us miserable. Our brains have to pile on huge amounts of pain to get anywhere near normal.

What's behind this is dopamine, a hormone produced by our brains. Dopamine is sometimes mischaracterised as a pleasure molecule. It's actually a motivator. If we keep our dopamine levels above our baseline, we feel joy, and we are motivated to learn and grow. We get things done. If it drops below that baseline, we feel anxious and struggle to focus. And if we remain down there we lack the motivation to do anything at all.

What's more, we develop our priorities based on the amount of dopamine we can expect in return for a particular action. If we become conditioned to expect just a little from a behaviour, we don't feel as compelled to do it. If, on the other hand, we expect a *lot* of dopamine, we are very motivated to take that action and repeat it over and over again. The primitive parts of our brains don't care if the activity is good for us; they just want the reward. High-sugar foods, social media and pornography release a lot of dopamine, making us very motivated towards them. Difficult, worthy and hard endeavours release less, and as a result we are less motivated to do them.

We are living in a world of abundance with brains wired for scarcity. You drink a beer, it feels good; then it doesn't anymore, so you drink another; then it doesn't feel good anymore, so you drink another, and another.

Here's where neuroadaptation kicks in. The primitive parts of our brains can't handle the amount of dopamine we're hitting them with. The normal back-and-forth seesawing isn't working, so it leaves a pile-up of gremlins on the pain side — changing the position of the middle point. We are now sitting in a base state of dissatisfaction; the balance is off. Our tolerance builds with each repeat of a similar stimulus, so the pleasure blast gets weaker and shorter and the pain response gets stronger and longer. You get a large increase in the desire to do the initial pleasurable behaviour, and less dopamine reward for doing it. It gets harder and harder to stop, and you feel less and less satisfied. The base state is now anxiety, irritability, insomnia, dysphoria, depression, boredom and craving. Pleasure becomes harder to come by. In short, our primitive brains were not wired for a convenient world, and we're suffering as a result of all this feel-good stuff. In affluent countries it's no longer just the rich and famous who indulge to dangerous levels. High-dopamine substances and behaviours are cheap and available; we all get to hammer the pleasure side of our reward centres to the point of dissatisfaction.

Anna Lembke believes that if we want to get out of this cycle, we should cut out as many feel-good substances and behaviours as we can, and do this for long enough for the system to rebalance itself to a more tranquil pain–pleasure ratio. The goal is to make the gremlins lose interest and leave the pain side of the seesaw. If we get ourselves unstimulated enough, the difficult, healthy things become fun again. Lembke recommends that depressed, anxious, irritable people cut out their feel-good drugs, foods and behaviours. Start by not staring at your phone, internet, games or filthy content for 24 hours; anything to recalibrate to a place where you can enjoy life. She calls this a dopamine detox — you avoid activities that cause sharp increases in pleasure. You might avoid things you crave, like fast food, ice cream and chocolate; no energy drinks, and definitely avoid cocaine and methamphetamines. You stay away from highly engaging activities like video games and social media. No gambling or excessive drinking. Engage only in low-stimulus activities. This will allow your brain to reset its dopamine levels, reducing your overall feelings of discomfort.

Ironically, leaning in to this more 'boring' existence will bring contentment to your life. Activities like productive work, spending time with the people you love, reading and eating healthily will become more enticing. They have now become rewarding enough for you.

So: if we are feeling bad, bored or dissatisfied, we should stop leaning in to so much pleasure. This is easy to do — unless of course, you are human, in which case it can be annoyingly hard to give up things you enjoy. That's where Judson Brewer can help.

HOW DO WE STOP?

Dr Judson Brewer is an American psychiatrist, scientist and author of *The Craving Mind*. He's had incredible success curbing bad habits. He has helped people out of their addictions to cocaine, meth, alcohol, screens and smoking, as well as pornography and food. Brewer studies the neural mechanisms of mindfulness (which means purposely bringing attention to the present experience), and he does this by using real-time functional magnetic resonance imaging (fMRI) to measure the small changes in blood flow that occur with brain activity. He's translated these fMRI findings into programmes to fight habits. If you are looking to stop doing something, *The Craving Mind* is a great place to start.

I zoomed Brewer at Brown University's Mindfulness Center to talk about how best to deal with our desires. On-screen he is a smiling picture of good health and enthusiasm. The guy loves this stuff.

Me: Judson, why can't we just will ourselves to stop doing things we know we shouldn't be doing?

Dr Jud: As much as we'd like to believe that willpower is powerful, it's more myth than muscle. In order to be able to break these habits, we have to use the powerful ancient parts of our brain. Willpower relies on the youngest, newest and weakest part of our brain, which ironically goes offline when we're stressed or anxious. We fall back into our old habit patterns when we're in those situations.

Me: So how do we stop then?

Dr Jud: Through the mechanism of being aware. You need three elements to form a habit: a trigger, a behaviour and a result. If we can pay attention and see very clearly what the result of a behaviour is, we can either reinforce a helpful habit or let go of an unhelpful one. That's why this process is called reward-based learning. If something's really rewarding, we're going to keep doing it. If it's not working, we can stop.

Awareness can help us pay attention and see how unrewarding some of these habits are. I've had plenty of patients come into my clinic who want to quit smoking. I tell them to go ahead and smoke, but this time clearly pay attention to the taste and experience as they smoke — and they realise the cigarettes taste like crap. When they realise that, they're less excited to smoke, and eventually they don't have to tell themselves to stop smoking. People can smoke a pack a day for years without ever really paying attention. When they do, they realise it's pretty disgusting.

That's how we change our habits. We become disenchanted with these old habits, and then we can replace those with healthier habits.

Me: So you teach your old brain that the habit doesn't help, and as a result it stops handing out the dopamine reward?

Dr Jud: Yes, I ask patients to be really curious. Use that curiosity to explore every physical sensation that comes up. That helps them not only foster the habit of being curious, but also helps them step out of the habit loop. Finally, it helps them see that these physical sensations pass. If you simply become aware of them and curious about them, they will go away. That is tremendously empowering.

You could try employing curiosity next time you're eating junk food. Take a single potato chip — before you put it in your gob, hold it up, look at it, smell it, and feel it on your fingers. When you finally place it carefully in your mouth, concentrate intently on the taste and the feel of the chip on your tongue. Become aware of all the sensations. Then zone right in as you crunch it with your teeth and swallow it. You will find it a very different experience than what you get when you mindlessly throw food down your throat. The flavour may be overwhelming. It may seem shockingly salty or even corrosive on your tongue. If you get curious about each chip you eat, you are unlikely to gobble a whole family-sized bag in one sitting.

Brewer teaches a bunch of practical tools to fight habits, including the R.A.I.N. technique inspired in part by Michele McDonald from Vipassana Hawai'i meditation centre. He took her Buddhist concept of R.A.I.N. and tested it with extensive neuroscientific research.

R.A.I.N. stands for Recognition, Acceptance, Interest and Note. Here's how it works.

- Desires pop up from the primal parts of our brain, triggered by past habit loops. To break these high-dopamine-reward cycles we need to listen to and then school our old brain. We can do this by riding that wave of craving until it passes.

- When a want appears in your mind, relax and RECOGNISE the desire. Rather than acting straight away, become aware of the want.
- Then ACKNOWLEDGE and accept it. Don't try to ignore it, don't try to distract yourself, but lean in to the desire. Think to yourself, 'Okay, I have a desire, here we go — let's ride this thing out.'
- Then jump on the mental wave by INVESTIGATING the craving as it builds. Judson suggests getting as curious as you can about everything that's happening at this point. Be aware of how your body and mind feel. All the sensations. Let them come to you. Tingling fingers, tightening tummy, swelling loins . . . closely experience everything. Follow those sensations intently until the craving subsides, which it does reasonably quickly. By concentrating on the desire, you have ridden it to shore.
- Then finally NOTE in your mind the most prominent sensation from the experience.

Any moment now you will probably have the desire to pick up your phone. You could use this as an opportunity to try out R.A.I.N. Follow the steps and ride out that craving.

I use the technique many times a day. I'll R.A.I.N. myself out of eating burgers, drinking or jumping on social media;

fighting cravings one by one as they arrive.

True change, however, only comes when we keep doing this. Every time we ride out our desires, we show the ancient lizard parts of our minds a new pathway. You have acknowledged the suggestion, so the brain has been heard. You have experienced the sensations created by that craving, but you have not acted. So you end up back to normal without going online, smoking, or doing whatever high-dopamine activity would have sent you crashing afterwards. And the brain registers that you didn't need to do what it told you to do. If you ride out the desire often enough, the lizard parts stop asking you to do that behaviour. They will likely look for something else to hassle you about, but if *that* habit isn't good for you then you can ride that one out, too.

If you are looking for a dopamine recalibration that will ultimately lead to a more satisfied life, you will need to ride out a bunch of habits as they arise. Eventually the good habits, like doing the work you need to do, or spending time with loved ones, will be the ones your brain pushes you towards.

* * *

> It is always by way of pain one arrives at pleasure.
>
> —Marquis de Sade, *Justine, or the Misfortunes of Virtue*, p. 179

Fighting off cravings is all very well and good, but life in our modern world is likely to be soft and comfortable whatever we do. There is a large amount of pleasure inherent in our day-to-day lives, especially when you compare us to the hard-living ancestors we evolved from. If pleasure is all around, you might get Dr Anna Lembke's 'gremlins' jumping on the pain side of your reward seesaw through no fault of your own.

So, what can we do about it? One way is to pursue pain and jolt the gremlins over to the pleasure side.

Whether it's the buzz we get from watching horror films, riding roller-coasters or getting tattooed, everyone has experienced pleasure post-pain. It's the logic behind ice baths and cold-water showers. After the initial shock you get, you experience a gradual increase in dopamine. Pleasure earns us pain, while pain earns us pleasure. It's a strange quirk of our existence that a bit of punishment makes life less punishing.

The way in which you create this pain is key. It would be counterproductive to walk around punching yourself in the face — you want to avoid anything that causes you actual physical damage. Luckily, there are highly effective low-impact ways to achieve positive results. The reward you get from a painful cold-water exposure can be equivalent to the rise you might experience snorting cocaine. However — unlike the drug — you don't get a large dopamine deficit from the cold water. The dopamine that comes with pain is indirect and, as such, is more enduring. There isn't an equal (or greater) and opposite negative reaction.

If you don't live near a naturally occurring cold-water source or have access to an ice bath, your shower is probably the best place to start. I start mine hot every morning and then shove it onto full cold for three minutes at the end: 90 secs hot, 180 as cold as it goes. I feel invigorated after I jump out, and over time I have come to look forward to that cold blast. On the odd occasion when I forget to do it, I feel sluggish in the morning. I crave that post-cold buzz so much that I'll turn my car air-conditioning to maximum while driving to work in the middle of winter to freeze myself out the best I can.

If you want to take this method deeper, you could investigate the work of Dutch breathing and ice-water enthusiast Wim Hof, also known as the 'Iceman'. He adds breathing techniques into the mix, taking the whole thing to the extreme. My cold-water adventures are more pedestrian; they are, however, strategic. If I need to do something intellectually or physically challenging but I'm struggling to find the motivation, I'll jump under (or into) some cold water. Afterwards, like clockwork, the thing I need to do becomes doable. A short, sharp shock leads to hours of productive behaviour. On the other hand, if I decide that first up I'll do an easier thing — or, worse, a pleasurable thing — it becomes even harder to do the hard thing. When there is a job to do, I suddenly feel the need to rearrange all the books on our shelves in descending order of size, attack my nose hairs with tweezers, clean under the couch cushions, make a snack or do some private browsing. This is because these things are easier than what needs to be done.

Cold water is also helpful on less worthy occasions. On the 1st January this year, after a massive New Year's Eve party, I woke up to find myself riddled with anxiety, impatience and a touch of self-hatred. So I stripped off, jumped into a freezing Lake Taupō and splashed around for ten minutes. It considerably improved my emotional state.

The enormous benefits that annoying people like me attribute to cold water have been questioned by some, and there's probably a significant placebo effect at play, but right now the pain-leads-to-pleasure part makes sense to me; it has changed my life, it's one of my 'pies' (see page 17) and I love it.

Another safe way to bring pleasure-inducing pain into your life is, of course, exercise. Going for a run is reasonably painful, but famously leads to a 'runner's high'. This can be seen as turning the temperature up on the gremlins. Any decent gym exercise, hill-walk, sport or hard physical work will do that same thing.

Yoga is an excellent example of how exertion leads to pleasure. The Yoga Sutra describes five different niyamas (positive duties or observances): saucha (cleanliness), santosha (contentment), tapas (self-discipline), svadhyaya (self-reflection), and ishvara pranidhana (surrender to a higher power). For me, yoga is a far shallower endeavour than that — I stretch to feel good.

In your typical Western commercial yoga session, you will perform 50 minutes of poses; some challenging, some gentle. You go through the Bridge, Triangle, Tree, Up Dog, Down Dog and Pigeon, among many others. You stretch, pull, strengthen and test yourself to your chosen limit. Then there is the sensational last ten minutes. Each session ends in a resting and restorative pose called Corpse or Savasana. After all the strenuous exercise, this downtime produces a euphoric, meditative mental and physical state. An intense feeling of wellbeing that continues as you roll up your mat, thank the instructor, walk out of the class and get in your car, and continues all the way home and long afterwards. Your efforts in your yoga class hurt enough that your brain balances that pain with a healthy flood of positivity and pleasure.

I originally saw yoga class as a way to improve strength, balance and flexibility — which it certainly does — but over time I have come to see it more as a means to reach tranquillity.

As I write this I have practised a minimum of half an hour of yoga every day for 248 days in a row. I was living life like a dry Weet-Bix, but now I get high on pain daily and I feel like I am made out of eels. I highly recommend the practice.

HAVING IT TOO GOOD

Why was I miserable in a movie theatre in Cologne when all my desires were being fulfilled? It was likely that the fulfilment of these desires was the very problem. As many a rock star has discovered, flash hotels, chauffeurs, parties, delicious food, booze, cocaine, meaningless sex and indulging in every other high-dopamine-producing behaviour we can doesn't make us as content as we might hope.

We don't instinctively know what makes us happy. In fact, we have it completely around the wrong way. We attempt to fill the holes in our hearts with things that create bigger holes. You don't have to be on a glamorous world tour for this to happen; the pleasure trap is cheap and available to everyone. Social media, junk food, video games and pornography are there for the taking. We have the opportunity to relentlessly slam the pleasure side all day, every day. And many of us have recalibrated ourselves to such a degree that we walk around at a default level set to 'miserable'.

The answer to this problem is also cheap. If we want to find a little peace and contentment, if we want to live a healthy life where wholesome, good and productive things become desirable, we need to embrace healthy pain and cut back on effortless highs. Exercise, hard work, and maybe a bit of cold water. If we learn to ride out our cravings for easy pleasure, the boredom, misery and dissatisfaction will recede. We might start walking around feeling a little less dissatisfied.

We might even find a way to enjoy and feel grateful for the good things in life, like being lucky enough to sit with a good friend in a packed movie theatre watching something you made together.

Chapter Three

Scared?

> Wild animals run from the dangers they actually see, and once they have escaped them worry no more. We however are tormented alike by what is past and what is to come. —Lucius Annaeus Seneca, *Moral Letters (Epistulae Morales)*, pp. 33–34

It's the winter of 2003, and a friend has scored me a job as the overnight security guard at an abandoned and allegedly haunted Victorian debtors' prison in London. A film crew is shooting till 9 p.m. each night and they need someone to stay over and watch the equipment until they return at 7 a.m.

The Whitecross Street Prison, or 'Cripplegate Coffeehouse' as it was known when it opened in 1815, quickly gained a grim reputation. Charles Dickens mentions the place in *The Posthumous Papers of the Pickwick Club* as an example of a particularly bad prison one should try to avoid being sent to. In eighteenth- and nineteenth-century England, destitute persons were incarcerated in debtors' prisons until they secured outside funds to repay the debts. There's an obvious catch-22 here — how do you make the money to get out while you're inside?

In 1847 journalist Nigel Cross wrote 'the crying evil of Cripplegate is that the unfortunate debtor had no means of protecting himself from association with the violently depraved'. In this building I am guarding tonight, hundreds of people once went insane and some took their own lives.

All this weighs on my mind as I trudge with my weak torch into the lower levels to make sure the film equipment hasn't been damaged by the water constantly dripping from the roof. They switch the power off at night, and the prison feels like a deep, dark tomb. Crawling through the rows of cells too small to stand in is bad, but wading through ankle-deep black water in the basement peaks my fear to new levels. My neck hairs are sticking straight up.

Then . . . I hear a splash in the far corner of the basement. I swing my dim torch wildly around, but see nothing. I ask — in a high-pitched squeak — 'Is anyone there?' Another splash; maybe a rat, maybe a poltergeist — I let the fear in and it takes over completely. A massive scream rings out, possibly from me but more likely from the tortured soul of an indebted Victorian pauper.

I run about five metres before tripping head-first into the cold water. The torch battery dies. My heart is pounding out of my chest. The ghoul draws nearer — I can definitely hear him now. He's stomping and splashing through the black water. Closer and closer.

Then I see him. Kind of. A split-second glimpse of a tall, pale-blue man with messy grey hair. I jump up and run towards a shimmer of grey light, scamper through it and bolt up the stairs, tripping multiple times before exploding out the big metal door onto the street, where I back onto the road and nearly get hit by a black cab. 'Get off the road, you absolute helmet!' the driver yells (or something similar).

Too scared to return, I abandon my post for a pub down the road and spend my entire £100 nightly prison pay drinking. In a drunken stupor, my mind circles back to that supernatural incident. Who — or what — tried to kill me?

Then it hits me. It was Christopher Walken from Tim Burton's 1999 supernatural horror flick *Sleepy Hollow*. In the movie he sports piercing, pale-blue eyes, yellow fangs, and a large black rider's coat with an ornate silver-metal armoured vest underneath. This all makes sense now. I'd seen the movie on DVD a week before while coming down off acid.

While it seems unlikely that Christopher Walken is actually lurking around in costume in the basement of a London debtors' prison, there's no way I can re-enter Cripplegate tonight; far too scared. When the pub closes, I take up a vigil down a nearby street, surveying the prison door like a trembling rabbit might watch a dog that wants to eat it.

This part of town is much more dangerous outside at night

on the street than locked in safely behind a large metal door. But such is the irrationality of fear.

At 6.59 a.m. I re-enter the prison, but only halfway into the entrance. The crew arrives, and I act as if I have been there all night discharging my responsibilities with honour.

The following evening, I bring a big black metal police torch for cracking ghost heads and a large bottle of Jack Daniel's for emotional support. The plan works: the more I drink, the less terrified I am. My cowardly, drunken approach gets me through, but I experience no pride. There has been no personal growth.

If I had faced my fears I might have become accustomed to the place, strengthened my character and built up my haunted-house bravery. I could have gained an ability not many people have. Instead I let fear, weakness, Cripplegate and, to a lesser extent, Christopher Walken win.

HOW FEAR WORKS

In 2022 I reached out via email to senior research fellow Dr Andrea Reinecke from the Department of Psychiatry at the University of Oxford and asked her what fear is. She told me it's

> the physiological and psychological response to a currently present threat stimulus, which initiates behavioural strategies that will protect us from getting harmed. As an example, an angry-looking large dog running towards us

> will trigger a fear reaction where we step aside. Anxiety is related to worries about imagined events or events in the future. —email interview, 19 July 2022

Remember the amygdala? The small, almond-shaped structure located deep within the temporal lobe of our brain, that's associated with anger (see Chapter One). It's also in the terror business. When a threat is detected, the amygdala triggers a fear response. Our bodies undergo near-instantaneous physical reactions designed to help us get away from a potential hazard. These include physiological changes like the release of stress hormones, as well as behaviours like freezing or fleeing. Our breathing becomes shallow and speeds up, our heart races, we jump and we flinch. Interestingly, the amygdala receives input not only from our eyes, ears and our sense of touch, but also from higher cognitive centres. So we can be fearful both of actual things and of things we imagine.

Fear emotions have obvious survival advantages, as they motivate us to take precautions. The fear of heights, fire and predators kept our ancestors alive long enough to reproduce. We are all descended from the scared humans who survived.

These days we experience comparatively few life-or-death situations, but we're still scared. We fear things that are unlikely to cause us physical harm, like public speaking, asking someone out or, for an increasing number of young people, the world outside our bedrooms. Left to fester, fears will grow into self-fulfilling loops, causing us to miss out on the good things in life. Fear can restrict our ability to experience human contact, love, adventure and so many other opportunities in life.

Fear emotions helped us get to the modern world, but to thrive in the here-and-now we need to accept that our biggest fears are probably all in our heads.

* * *

In his excellent book *The Expectation Effect*, UK science writer David Robson details a drone attack at London's Gatwick Airport. On 19 December 2018, a security guard reported two 'unmanned aerial vehicles' — one flying around the perimeter fence, another inside the complex. The airport was immediately locked down. Over the next few days, dozens of drones were sighted around the airport by multiple witnesses. Yet the police, airport security and the military couldn't locate any of these hostiles.

The panic grew. Over 170 sightings flooded in and alerts were sent out to other airports warning that similar attacks might occur. Around a thousand flights were cancelled, with 140,000 passengers disrupted — yet no evidence of any drones has ever been found. Despite offering a substantial reward, the police haven't got a culprit, or even a single photo offering evidence of an attack.

This wasn't a conspiracy, a practical joke or mass dishonesty.

It was simply the power of our expectations and fears to create visions. Much like Christopher Walken in a prison basement, the drones were never there.

I zoom Dave Robson at 4 a.m. New Zealand time. He's a smart, engaging, handsome and immaculately dressed man; I stay in bed, fake a bookshelf background and ask Dave where our phantom fears come from. Here's what he says:

> If you look at the wiring of the visual cortex at the back of the head, you'll find that the nerves bringing electrical signals from the retina are vastly outnumbered by the neural connections feeding in predictions from other regions of the brain. In terms of the data it provides, the eye is a relatively small (but admittedly essential) element of your vision, while the rest of what you see is created 'in the dark' within your skull.
>
> The brain is constantly simulating the world around it. Predicting what's going to happen in the next few seconds, next few minutes. These simulations shape the sensory processing of the information hitting our eyes and ears. It can shape that data. It can add things from its predictions and delete things that it doesn't think are relevant. Most of the time it works well. Sometimes it gets things very wrong and that can cause problems. Like unnecessary fears and stress responses.

Put simply, just because you have fears — even about things you see with your own eyes — it doesn't mean they are real. We should challenge all of them.

* * *

Thanks to social media, video games, food-ordering apps and adult entertainment, most of our human needs are accessible from our homes. Avoiding the fears that come with the real world is easier now than ever before. With a little bit of help, we can hide away from everything.

Unfortunately, the choices at our fingertips are seldom the healthy, meaningful ones. Over time, these easy options make life harder. Our brains are wired such that every time we avoid the real world, it becomes more difficult to rejoin it. For example, say you have a natural apprehension around social occasions. You might begin taking the easy option by not attending gatherings when invited. By doing this you teach your brain that this was the right thing to do. You didn't go out and meet people because you were scared to do it, and then you didn't die — so your brain assumes that the decision to stay home was the right one; that it kept you alive. It then strengthens your social apprehension to keep you from harm; this makes it a little harder to go out the next time.

Keep giving in to your fear and avoiding human interactions long enough, and a small concern can turn into a full-blown phobia. Dr Andrea Reinecke puts it this way:

> Fears worked well when getting us away from a steep cliff or a hungry sabre-toothed tiger. But it can get out of control when stimuli or situations land in the threat category that don't belong there. Your amygdala might be 'saying' safe social situations are terrible and might even tell you to avoid them; so you avoid that social situation. You get an invite, you don't go. You stay at home. But your amygdala will now strengthen that social fear, because you have not died — to the amygdala this is surely only because you avoided the situation. —email interview, 19 July 2022

This is why it's a bad idea to blindly follow the whims of your primitive lizard brain. It doesn't have all the information. It doesn't know that restricting socialisation can lead to depression. It doesn't care that staying home might cause you to miss out on meeting your soul-mate, a person who could have made your life happy and meaningful. The primitive part of the brain needs to be shown that these things are safe so it can take them off its terror list. As Dr Reinecke puts it:

> It's about testing whether what your brain tells you is threatening really is threatening. Teaching the amygdala that going to that lunch won't kill you. —email interview, 19 July 2022

Cognitive behavioural therapy, or CBT, is a psychological intervention that aims to reset the brain by disproving the catastrophic outcomes of a scenario. In standard CBT you would see a therapist eight to twelve times, gradually approaching the situations you are afraid of. At Oxford, Dr Reinecke does it all in a single session. She believes in a 'rip the band-aid off' approach to fear, and it's getting amazing results. As she explains:

> We send the message that we are absolutely convinced that nothing terrible will happen, no matter how hard they push — so we drop all safety strategies in one go, as far as that is possible. If you are scared to catch a bus, we face this in a slightly bizarre 'get on that bus and drop dead' fashion. Our work shows that even very brief treatment reduces the amygdala hypersensitivity to a healthy level — within 24 hours of treatment.
> —email interview, 19 July 2022

Basically, if you are claustrophobic, then you need to spend fifteen minutes in a cupboard to show your brain that small spaces won't kill you. This is pretty much what Dr Andrea does in her research. She puts people who are scared to be in tiny rooms in tiny rooms — and it works. They don't die, and as a result they become less scared. Conversely, every time you avoid a small space, a social occasion or a spider out of fear, you are proving the amygdala right and your fear grows stronger and becomes harder to face. The sooner we aggressively face our fears, the better. When it doesn't hurt you, the fear shrinks away and adventure, opportunity and pride grow.

This is not to say that we should throw caution completely to the wind. The famous Vegas big-cat tamers Siegfried and Roy enjoyed a lucrative career until 3 October 2003, when lack of fear cost Roy dearly. On stage that evening, he tried something more daring than usual with a giant, seven-year-old white tiger named Mantacore. The big cat slashed up the tan German birthday boy, ripping open multiple parts of his body, unleashing a torrent of blood onto the stage and severing Roy's spine. Thankfully, modern medicine was on hand to save the entertainer's life.

While some fears are silly, others are smart. It makes sense to remain careful around giant predators, speeding cars and knife-wielding maniacs — but not so much public speaking, socialising and ghosts. While there *are* things out there that we should be cautious of, just because you have a fear of something doesn't mean you should avoid that thing. We should question all of our fears.

THINGS WE FEAR AND HOW TO DEAL WITH THEM

In his 1998 comedy special *'I'm Telling You for the Last Time'*, Jerry Seinfeld points out that some people list public speaking as their number one fear — above death. So, at a funeral they would prefer to be in the coffin rather than delivering the eulogy . . .

Public speaking can give us a huge advantage in life. When you can confidently address a crowd, you set yourself apart from those who shy away from the opportunity. So why not go for it? I mean, what's the worst that could happen?

In September 2022, former Japanese prime minister Shinzo Abe was gunned down while delivering a speech at a road junction near the north exit of Yamato-Saidaiji Station in Nara City. Abe was pronounced dead at the hospital five and a half hours after being shot. If that morning he had experienced a fear of public speaking, it would have proved justified. *That's* the worst that could happen.

Luckily, you and I (probably) aren't prominent or important enough to worry about assassination. You might metaphorically die on stage, but your work-mates are unlikely to shoot you.

As he explains on the website Psychology Today, physicist, futurist and executive management consultant Dr Karl Albrecht believes there are five types of human fear that we all share. The fear of ceasing to exist. The fear of losing any part of our precious bodily structure. Loss of autonomy — the fear of being immobilised, paralysed, restricted. Separation — the fear of abandonment, rejection. Ego-death — the fear of humiliation.

Fear of public speaking fits nicely into the Ego-death category, along with a sniff of Separation. Speaking in front of people brings with it risk and reward in terms of social status.

If you excel behind the lectern, your stocks rise; people push to talk to you afterwards, organisers are thankful, that special someone in the crowd is impressed. Fail, and you will feel like your stocks have plummeted. However, to get to the point where you can succeed, you have to risk failure as often as you can. You need to challenge your fear system and prove it wrong. If you don't physically die then you can do it again, and each time you survive you grow less scared.

When it comes to the first steps of public speaking, American neuroscientist Ethan Kross, author of *Chatter: The voice in our head (and how to harness it)*, discusses a technique from his research which he calls 'distanced self-talk'. The idea is to talk to yourself as if you were a friend. For example, before any public speaking engagement I might tell myself: 'Matt, you have your notes, you know what you are going to say, you are going to be fine, buddy.' Kross conducted an experiment with volunteers divided into two groups. One group focused on their fears using first-person pronouns, while the other group 'distanced' themselves by using their own name. The second group reported less shame and embarrassment, ruminated less about their performance afterwards and, according to a panel of judges, delivered better speeches. Kross believes that using your own name when talking to yourself creates emotional distance and allows you to gain perspective.

Maybe your path to facing this fear starts with a few words on special occasions in front of friends and family. Soon you're speaking up at work; eventually you can face rooms, halls, stadiums. A whole world opens up to you because you faced a fear. Before long, you enjoy the thing you were terrified of so much that no one can shut you up. A boss of mine once delivered seven full speeches at a work Christmas party. I'd prefer it if that guy had a bit of public-speaking fear in his system.

* * *

In 1975, the biggest movie in the world was *Jaws*. A beautifully shot, carefully crafted flick that ruined swimming for a generation of kids. Like many New Zealanders, I think about sharks a lot, and not just in the ocean. Sharks pop into my brain in freshwater lakes and chlorinated central Auckland pools. I don't believe they're there, but they are in my thoughts anyway.

On one level, a fear of sharks makes sense. They have big teeth that could bite your leg off and leave you bleeding to death. This has certainly happened to people. But the odds of being attacked by a shark are minimal: the ISAF (International Shark Attack File — I kid you not) recorded 73 shark attacks globally in 2021, of which nine were fatal. On the other hand, the chance of a shark being attacked by a human are much higher. We kill 100 million of their kind a year. That's 11,000 sharks per hour, or three per second. In the shark *vs* man battle of the species, they should be very scared of us. But, of course, fears aren't always logical.

A few years ago I was fishing on a friend's boat with my eleven-year-old son. He was pulling a snapper out of the water when a three-metre-long mako jumped up and bit the fish right off his line. It freaked the hell out of us. The next day, while snorkelling, my boy asked if we were in the same water as that shark that stole his snapper. In a shaky voice, I told him that, technically, we were. If you think about it, all the oceans and seas are linked together. We are in the same water as all the sharks in the world. I quickly bustled my boy back into the boat and we sped off.

On the way home, guilt replaced fear. I realised that my irrational thinking around sharks was impacting my son's ability to enjoy the water. We'd missed out on a day's snorkelling because of this weakness of mine. Something needed to be done.

When we got home, I got myself a ticket to the Shark Cage Adventure at Kelly Tarlton's (a low-level indoor version of what they do out at sea in the Foveaux Strait with the great white sharks). A few days later — in a state of intense fear — I climbed into the indoor tank with a guide and some buddies from *The Matt & Jerry Show* on Radio Hauraki. We floated around in a cage letting all the big sharks check us out.

A funny thing happens when you're 20 centimetres from a massive tiger shark for an extended period of time. It changes before your eyes from a terrifying monster into a big fish. There have been zero problems with sharks since. I won't be covering myself in fish guts and jumping into the middle of an active great white breeding ground anytime soon, but the world's waters are now considerably more open to me and my son.

* * *

The fear of needles and injections also makes sense on some level. Before modern medicine, letting the outside world into your bloodstream was a terrible idea. Cuts could lead to blood-poisoning. Even little pricks from mosquitoes could bring malaria and death.

Nowadays — as long as you know what's in the needle — the fear isn't so rational. Still, many of us remain terrified. The mother of my children is a brave person. She can drop into a half-pipe, skydive and gave birth to two beautiful oversized baby boys, yet she screams and runs off if you mention an injection. I'm with her — I would rather be punched in the face by a nurse than have her prick my arm. When it comes to major dentistry work, it's not the teeth being ripped from the gums that concerns people like me: it's the little injections of local anaesthetic at the start.

This fear needs to be faced. What better way to do that than giving blood? So I book in a donation at our local New Zealand Blood Service. Leaning in to Dr Andrea Reinecke's lessons, I resolve to tackle my dread by experiencing every aspect of the skin-piercing insertion. In the past I have distracted myself when injections were involved. It seemed like a common-sense approach: if you are scared of needles, the natural reaction is to look away. Squeeze your fists. Clench your teeth. But the thing is, *Jaws* is scarier because we hardly see the shark: in a movie that's over two hours long, he appears for less than four minutes. It's the same with jabs — the fear grows more powerful if we don't face it.

As the needle cuts through my flesh, I channel Shinzen Young. In the late 1960s, this man — who was to become a Shingon Buddhist monk — moved into a tiny, unheated, isolated ice-shack near the Mount Kōya temple settlement in Wakayama Prefecture, south of Osaka. He lived there on his own for 100 days, spending his time dousing himself with litres of bone-chilling melted snow. Shinzen dealt with this by learning to exist completely in the moment. At first he shied away from the painful experiences of his isolation. But he soon realised that the problem wasn't the activities themselves but his attempts to not experience them. When he stopped blocking out the sensations and instead began focusing intently on them, his discomfort was greatly eased.

And so, in a blood donation lab, determined to conquer my fear, I focus my attention entirely on the fat needle piercing my skin. Like the wuss I am, every fibre of me screams 'LOOK AWAY!', but I do not. I hold my nerve as the blood flows. I stare directly at it and concentrate completely on what is going on. I am aware of every sensation. The pain turns out to be so minor that it's almost disappointing; more of a numbness than anything. There is nothing to fear. When it's over, like magic my dread of injections is gone, almost entirely. I kind of enjoyed it.

There are, of course, people who love needles too much. I have known some heroin enthusiasts in my time. That is a different set of problems.

RETURN TO PRISON

In October 2023 I revisit the terrifying Cripplegate Prison in London, along with my little sister Imogen and her partner, Rob. After years of thinking ill of this place and telling anyone who would listen the story of the horrors I had faced in there, I have to say: it's just a building. It's not even a very impressive one. From the street, the only thing that gives any hint of its debtors' prison past is a small blue circular plaque on its nice orange-brick walls. This reads:

> English Hedonists
> Whitecross Debtors' Prison, 1813–1870
>
> Warm-hearted Nell Gwynne, in her will, desired her natural son, the Duke of St. Albans, to lay out £20 a year to release poor debtors out of prison, and this sum was distributed every Christmas Day to the inmates of Whitecross Street Prison.
>
> Made in England

This time I am not alone and I don't stay over, but *boy* has Cripplegate grown larger and more evil in the remembering. The metal prison door which I burst out of onto the street in terror all those years ago does not resemble the gates of Arkham Asylum as I remember. It is, in reality, a slightly-smaller-than-usual street-level entrance with someone's half-arsed tag 'Dupa' sprayed on the front. There are no imposing stone steps leading down to a terrifying Jack the Ripper-style cobbled street, as I have described it to everyone. This is a small exit opening on to a quaint little road featuring some nice cafes and bars. No horror show this time; just a charming area on a warm autumn evening. We stop for a beer at the pub where I'd hidden trembling in fear all those years ago. It's lovely.

Maybe the prison is still terrifying underground, in the cells. I get down on the ground and stare in through the barred street-level windows, but I don't get poltergeist vibes. No wraith with piercing pale-blue eyes and yellow fang-like teeth looking out at me. There is nothing here that would require running and screaming.

On top of this supposedly evil building sit some nice apartments. People live their day-to-day lives above this old prison. I couldn't even handle one night in there without a bottle of Jack Daniel's. Pathetic. What a wuss. My sister, who has heard my scary prison-job story a number of times, can't help but smile. 'This is the place you won't shut up about?' One thing is for sure, I won't be sharing the 'terrifying' tale of my time at Cripplegate Prison anymore. Most of it was in my head.

Chapter Four

Lonely?

A convertible Audi with two bikini-clad models in the back seat is parked by a large jump ramp on a giant sound stage at 3 Mills Studios, East London. A six-foot ape is wrestled into a large rectangular cage beside the car. Fifty metres from this, a drunk moustachioed stuntman mounts his bike. On paper, the stunt looks good. There are four camera crews situated on giant towers, dozens of oversized New Zealand flags, and hundreds of fireworks ready to blow.

The problem is in the cage: the ape isn't angry enough. Luckily, with seconds to go, safety coordinator Dick Johansonson soaks the ape in gasoline and sets fire to the beast with a cigarette. The ape is now furious. It screeches and thrashes around violently. Randy pedals hard and hits the ramp at pace, the fireworks explode across the arena, audience members grimace: is he going to make it? No! The stunt goes horribly wrong — Cambell crashes violently on top of the cage, which collapses, trapping the burning ape inside.

Unfortunately for me, the burning ape isn't really an ape; it's me in a highly flammable monkey suit. Our crew, dubbed 'Back of the Y', are shooting a Randy Cambell stunt for the UK TV show *Balls of Steel* starring director and stuntman Chris Stapp in the titular role. Interestingly, throughout this dangerous fracas, my primary emotion isn't fear or excitement: it's loneliness. I've been stuck in London on my own for months. I desperately miss my girlfriend, who's back home in New Zealand.

I finally break out from the cage, but now I can't see out of my monkey-suit eye-holes; instead of running towards the safety of the extinguishing pool, I run straight towards the terrified studio audience. Despite this precarious situation, I'm completely consumed by that empty, removed-from-reality sensation you get when you become socially disconnected. As my burn time hits two minutes and the pain at the back of my neck becomes unbearable, I suddenly get smashed from behind. It's a beautiful, life-saving tackle from the *real* stunt coordinator that slams me into the extinguishing water.

That night, after a few drinks during which no one seems to talk to me, I taxi home by myself, climb up to the roof of my apartment building and sit there. With the smell of burnt fake monkey and real human skin hanging in the air, I contemplate the day's success and how far we have come from our humble beginnings in New Zealand. There is a lot to be proud of. I smile, and think to myself: 'I'm so fucking lonely. Maybe I should slide off the roof and see what happens.'

Loneliness is such a painful and powerful emotion, you can experience it at the peak of your career, surrounded by people, and even while you are on fire in a monkey suit.

* * *

Psychiatrist Robert Waldinger is the director of the Harvard Study of Adult Development where he runs the most comprehensive longitudinal happiness study ever undertaken. Waldinger, his staff and their predecessors have been following 1000 Bostonians across their entire adult lives. After analysing tens of thousands of pages of information, blood samples and DNA tests and running millions of hours of interviews across 75 years, Waldinger shared this simple message to a packed crowd in a TED talk at the Beacon Street Auditorium:

> Good relationships keep us happier and healthier. Period.

When asked how to achieve these relationships, he suggests focusing on people instead of screens. Going on long walks and date nights; letting go of feuds and keeping in touch with family members.

According to Waldinger and his massive study, satisfaction with life largely comes from the interactions we have with the people around us. At age 50, things like cholesterol levels weren't the key indicator of how well you age; it was the quality of relationships. Those who were happiest with the people around them at 50 were the most healthy at 80. Good-quality human interaction over a lifespan was associated with stronger brain and physical health. Not only did people with mates, close family and partners live longer, but they also experienced less pain when sick or injured. Those who retired and made the effort to reach out to new people did particularly well. When they were young adults, most of the people in the study believed that wealth, fame and professional success would lead to the good life. That isn't how it panned out; those who did the best later on were the ones who put effort into their relationships.

Another finding from this study will surprise very few. It turns out that a focus on drinking, drugs, junk food and easy options did not lead to a happier life for the participants.

Of course, it's all very well saying you need great relationships — but how do you get them and keep them? This is something humans have been working on for a very long time.

* * *

We are relatively slow-moving, small-toothed and thin-skinned creatures. Our ancestors didn't last very long when they found themselves on their own, but together we have proven hard to beat. With friends and family on our side we became incredible hunters, gatherers, builders, fighters and parents. It's a question of survival. While foals, calves and pups are up and about in minutes after birth, our children remain helpless and dependent for years. Escaping the jaws of sabre-toothed tigers and dire-wolves was challenging enough with our sluggish human legs, but near-impossible with a baby or two on the hip. We needed each other.

The survival advantages of group behaviour were so strong that it led to the development of loneliness — a painful emotional warning that urges us to stay close to others and to work on social connections. Early humans who didn't experience this emotion tended to drift off and get eaten, or starve to death, or fall in holes they couldn't get out of. The ones with a strong desire to stick together thrived.

Loneliness works in the same way that sensations like thirst and hunger do. They motivate us to behave in ways that help us survive and pass on our genes. As John T. Cacioppo and colleagues explain in the paper 'Evolutionary mechanisms for loneliness':

> . . . loneliness is an aversive state that motivates us to take action that minimizes damage.

These days, going solo isn't nearly as dangerous. Tigers seldom get into our homes and rip out our throats as we sleep. Yet we are the same creatures. We feel isolation as keenly as we did when our physical survival depended on togetherness. Nowadays, ironically, our powerful emotion of loneliness can become the danger in itself. It can cause the release of the same hormones that fire us up in times of peril. If they stick around too long, this can put pressure on our cardiovascular system and lead to unhealthy inflammation in our body. In short, things don't go well if we live in a constant state of loneliness-induced fight or flight. As social cognitive neuroscientist Matthew Lieberman points out in his book *Social: Why our brains are wired to connect*, loneliness

> damages tissues and blood vessels and increases the risk of heart disease and other chronic illnesses. Loneliness leads to changes in gene expression in white blood cells, which in turn results in reduced defences against viruses. (p. 73)

The US National Institute on Aging has suggested that the health risks of prolonged isolation may be equivalent to smoking fifteen cigarettes a day. Social isolation and loneliness have been estimated to shorten a person's lifespan by as much as fifteen years. Today, people who are socially isolated experience increased risk of stroke, heart disease, mental health disorders and a variety of premature mortalities. Few things in life are more important to our physical and mental health than strong connections with family and friends. Yet many of us don't prioritise our relationships with others. We treat our social life like a 'nice to have'.

Imagine a drug that decreases the risk of premature death, lowers inflammation, protects you from heart disease and obesity, fights depression, lowers anxiety and reduces tissue damage. This drug also makes you laugh hysterically, helps you move house, and you can play golf with it, cuddle it and even make love to it. These are all benefits of human interaction. If it were a drug, we'd be injecting, snorting and smoking that thing constantly.

* * *

Unfortunately, we don't get all the benefits of togetherness simply by being near other humans. We are quite capable of experiencing intense loneliness in a busy office, at a party, or burning alive in an ape suit in front of a live studio audience.

Swiss psychiatrist and psychotherapist Carl Jung (1875–1961) described this human dilemma:

> Loneliness does not come from having no people about, but from being unable to communicate the things that seem important to oneself. —in *Memories, Dreams, Reflections*, p. 240

If we want the full health and mental wellbeing benefits of human companionship, we need people we can confide in, depend on and trust. It doesn't matter *how* many other humans are around us — if we don't connect with them, we feel lonely. It's the loneliness that's the problem, not the aloneness. While some of us can't stand being alone for a single night, others do very well by themselves. Some relish it. Take Andrew Fagan, a well-known and much-loved New Zealander who has experienced huge popularity and played to massive crowds across his career. The man has created so many great songs, including hits with The Mockers like 'Forever Tuesday Morning', 'Swear It's True' and 'Seven Years Not Wasted'. He has spent a lot of his life with an audience, but he also enjoys time spent completely alone at sea. Fagan has written two excellent sailing-themed autobiographies, *Swirly World: The solo voyages* and *Swirly World Sails South*, about his adventures. He heads out for months at a time, dealing with storms, seasickness, safety and constipation on the high seas. His last offshore solo sailing experience, in 2022, turned into a biblical 40 days and 40 nights. The thought of spending this much time alone in peril terrifies me, so I reached out to the man via email for an explanation.

Me: What attracts you to spending time alone?

Andrew: Being in a self-contained capsule on the sea and using the wind alone to travel where you want to is an all-consuming, wonderful thing. There is so much sensory stimulus with wind and sea-state changes. The sea when agitated by the wind can become so huge and dangerous and exciting all at the same time. It can be compelling, but at times boring as well. It all depends on what the wind wants to do.

Me: Is loneliness a big part of the challenge?

Andrew: There's a difference between loneliness and aloneness. Aloneness is the prized ongoing experience at sea in an invigorating, unpredictable saline environment. You are sailing by yourself surrounded by a three-sixty horizon with nothing on it. The total focus is on keeping the boat sailing where you want to go.

Aloneness and the necessity for personal survival decision-making is all-consuming. Prolonged aloneness thousands of miles away from land is not as bad as some may think.

Me: What is it like to see people again after being alone for so long?

Andrew: Re-discovering human-inhabited land is an intoxicating experience. The longer you spend alone out of sight of land, the more you value the return. And because you are sailing slowly, the land that wasn't on the horizon but now is may take many sailing hours to slowly close in with. It all depends on the wind strength and direction. That slow, tantalising sailing approach builds suspense. And when you've usually been awake for much longer than you should be, the whole experience becomes surreal. Out of it for free.

Fagan, meditating monks and long-haul truckers aside, most people struggle on their own for large stretches of time. This inability to operate solo may well be a weakness that more of us should test; but over the long term, life is richer, fuller, healthier and happier for most of us when we have people we love around. It's good to have mates.

* * *

In 2019, in a real-life equivalent of the 2009 movie *I Love You, Man*, UK author Max Dickins was about to propose to his girlfriend when he realised he didn't have any mates good enough to be the best man. For years he had been splitting his time between his work, his partner and his family. Somewhere along the line he'd lost his circle of friends. Max knew a lot of people, but few of them well.

When he looked into the problem, he discovered that more and more people are ending up in the same boat. So he wrote *Billy No-Mates*, an investigation into the dire state of male friendships in modern Western societies.

I zoomed Max at his London home and we talked for well over an hour. He's the kind of guy I could totally be buddies with.

Me: Are we more socially disconnected today, and if so why?

Max: Yes, we are. Particularly men. A mental health charity asked men, in the UK, how many close friends they have. One in three had none. They also asked them how many people they could talk to about a medical, personal or work problem. Half of them had no one.

There is a thing social scientists call 'network shrinkage'. As we get older, our social circle decreases. Men's get a great deal smaller than women's do. A big thing is the way we are around one another. We use banter. Joshing, ribbing, taking the piss. It's great fun, but it doesn't necessarily create a culture where we feel we have permission to take friendship beyond fun. To move it to a deeper, lasting level. Men often don't show their full self because it would give mates ammo. Competition and hierarchies are very important to men. We are concerned with status, so we may not admit when things aren't great. Plus there's a taboo against showing affection. We struggle with something as simple as telling a mate we like them.

Me: Why do women tend to hold on to connections with friends and family, where men might not?

Max: Female friendships tend to be face-to-face, based around talk. There's a lot of emotional disclosure. Male friendships tend to be side-by-side, based around sharing space, sharing activities, often in groups. This might be

> why male friendships are less close and why they struggle to last compared to female ones. Everyone is different, but it seems on balance male friendships work better when they involve doing something physical. Golf, building, hunting, tinkering. We struggle to feel comfortable face-to-face unless we are doing something or if there is drinking involved, which — while fun — can be a bit of a crutch.

So, if we accept that life is better with deeper connections, how do we go about getting them?

After a year of trying to make friends, Max found that the best strategy was the most obvious one. Show up in places where you can actually meet people. Gyms, sports teams, cooking classes, clubs, games nights. Anywhere you might come across like-minded people — or, if you are getting desperate, *any* people. Max talks about a lonely friend who started turning up at weekly military board-games evenings. He found a bunch of new friends. That may seem boring to you, but that guy and his new mates love it. Actually meeting up is key. Social media is one thing; but, according to Max, being there in person is hugely important. It's how friendships move up a notch.

When it comes to the close friends we already have, it may feel like they are with us forever — but they can easily slip away. Deeper, long-term friendships involve effort. Many of us neglect friends or keep them at arm's length. Max argues that nurturing friendships is as important as finding friends in the first place.

Max: When you emerge from your twenties, you can't rely on spontaneity anymore. Especially if you have a family. When it comes to close friends, the regularity of the contact and the intensity of it is really important. If you don't see them, you're not gonna maintain that closeness. So whether it's a poker night every fortnight or a five-a-side football league with a beer afterwards, regularity is really important so you don't have to reinvent the wheel. If you're a bloke, activities work the best.

It's important to do the work of being the friend; literally, the admin, the emotional work of being the one that shows up, checks in. The best way to have friends is to be a friend. Can you make your friendships a little bit closer? You don't have to become a wishy-washy new man, but you can expand your toolbox.

Do you have enough relational skills in your box to have the conversations you need to foster a close friendship? You can do banter, but can you go vulnerable when needed? When someone is disclosing something to you, can you respond in kind to make them feel better? Can you listen? Can you ask great questions? Work on these things, and your friendships become closer and more fulfilling. They will also endure.

There are simple things we can do to move friendships up to a more meaningful level. The most obvious is paying attention to others. Focusing on what people are saying rather than doing what we usually do, which is zone out while we wait for them to stop speaking so we can punish them with another amazing story about ourselves. We sit in our own thoughts most of the day. It seems like a waste to remain there when we have someone in front of us. Relationships grow when we choose to engage. It feels good to listen and react to someone else for a change.

Dr Vivek Murthy, the twenty-first Surgeon General of the United States and the author of *Together: The healing power of human connection in a sometimes lonely world*, points out something we all know to be true: there is little point in going through the effort of organising a face-to-face hang-out only to spend it staring down at your phone. We've all done this. You are with a friend, talking, it's great to see them and then suddenly you feel the deep need to message someone else, check social media, look up the name of an actor in a movie. Once the phone is in your hand, you're completely focused on your device and not on your buddy. Seeing that you have abandoned them, your friend takes the opportunity to jump on their phone, too. You are now sitting across from each other focusing on people who aren't there with you. Yet if we give each other our full attention, a meet-up becomes so much more meaningful and fun. We are unlikely to take friendships to new, deeper levels mid-scroll.

A stark example of the public isolation we impose on

ourselves can be seen in footage taken on the Champs-Élysées in Paris during the New Year's Eve countdown to 2024. As a big digital display ticks down to midnight, a sea of people face the Arc de Triomphe, but no one watches with their own eyes. No one has their arm around the person beside them; no one is talking. In a scene reminiscent of a dystopian movie, every one of the thousands of people there stares into near-identical rectangular devices held out in front of them. When the clock reaches 2024 and the fireworks blast, no one hugs, claps, kisses or interacts with the people around them. They just stand there viewing events digitally. They may be filming the beautiful event to view later, to gain a few likes when they post it, or to prove they were there. What they are not doing is experiencing the moment meaningfully with the other human beings around them.

UNHAPPY ENDING

An increasing number of people in modern Western societies are disconnecting completely from friends and family as they grow old. On its website, the New Zealand Citizens Advice Bureau provides the grim details of what happens to your body if you die alone.

> When the authorities have determined that there is no next of kin, they will release the body from the mortuary and into the care of a funeral director. The

> funeral director then must apply to the local council for an 'indigent funeral' grant and make a statutory declaration that there is no one available to pay the funeral fees. The grant covers the cost to the funeral director of providing a basic casket and delivering the deceased to the crematorium or cemetery. The grant does not cover the cost of a gravestone.

Death is the easy part here — the years spent completely on your own beforehand are the real challenge. In August 2023 I read this shocking line in an *Otago Daily Times* report on the sorry state of the elderly in Dunedin:

> In one boarding house, tenants talked of a resident's body discovered days after death 'dissolved into the mattress'. —Mary Williams, 'Exposed: Abandoned in Dunedin's houses of horror'

So how do you prevent yourself from ending up alone, melted into your bed? Well, if you are lucky enough to have a partner or friends and family, you could stick with them through thick and thin, good and bad, stinky and clean. Barring toxic, dangerous relationships, you may want to do whatever it takes to keep these people around.

In his book *Four Thousand Weeks: Time management for mortals*, Oliver Burkeman argues that magazines and inspirational social media memes have it wrong when they tell us not to settle for what we have. He believes we absolutely should. Burkeman points out that choosing not to settle is usually a form of settling in itself. You may decide that the person you are with isn't as good as the infinite possibilities out there. With a fantasy in mind, you embark on ten frustrating years swiping away on dating apps looking for someone better. That's settling, too: you have opted to spend a large amount of your finite time on this planet doing something that is less than ideal.

Australian National University professor of philosophy Robert E. Goodin wrote an entire book focused on the positives of settling (called, unsurprisingly, *On Settling*). He believes that to have a fulfilling relationship, we must settle for a period of time on an imperfect person. To do this we have to stop fixating on all the incredible alternatives we imagine are out there. If you find a good person, let them in; and once they are in, stand by them. Often, however, we leave partners or let a friendship slide for nothing more than their crime of imperfection. When it comes to our lovers, we fail to commit because we feel like we are missing out on something. Our partners have to compete with the gods and goddesses we believe we deserve. As Burkeman points out, we look for traits in our fantasy romantic partners that can't possibly exist in one person; for example, someone who is simultaneously incredibly exciting and very stable. When our current partner doesn't pull off this impossible feat, we decide it's their fault and start looking for someone who can.

If you spend your life searching for a person who doesn't exist, you're going to spend a serious amount of time on your own. In his life-changing book *The Course of Love*, British author Alain de Botton argues that it is infantile to expect someone to be 'simultaneously a best friend, a lover, a co-parent, a co-chauffeur and a business partner' (p. 162). This idea leads to resentment and disappointment and ruins marriages that could otherwise have been fruitful and rewarding.

A partner doesn't need to fill all of these roles in your life. Your mates can be your best mates, your business partner your business partner, and your lover your lover. All you have to do is find someone you like who loves you and you love back. Once you've done this, settle.

Burkeman believes that not only should we look to settle, but we should do it in a way that makes it harder to back out. Moving in together, kids, marriage. You only have so much time in the world to build a life, so lock in some people around you and share what little you have with them. We end up happier when we give up the fantasy life and get busy living our real one.

Of course, the big relationships aren't the only human connections we have in life. In a podcast on the website Hidden Brain, Dr Vivek Murthy explains how the secondary connections we make in our wider communities are also important for our wellbeing. These are the people in your neighbourhood, workplace and the cafes you visit. The one-off but meaningful chats you can have with Uber drivers or people behind counters.

He suggests that we make the effort to greet, acknowledge and check in on as many people as we can. That we are hard-wired for this kind of compassionate communication and, as such, it is good for our bodies and minds.

Despite their best efforts, though, some people may struggle to connect. Others tragically lose the people they have chosen to settle with. But luckily, even in the most dire of circumstances, we don't have to be completely alone.

* * *

This may sound glib, but you can always get a pet. They may not be as effective at fighting loneliness as getting a human, but they're pretty good. A 2019 study published in the journal *BMC Public Health* by Lauren Powell and colleagues confirmed something that many of us knew already: dogs make great buddies. They found that new dog owners felt less lonely soon after getting the dog, and stayed that way for as long as they were in the study.

As it turns out, dogs are potent human wellbeing generators. American neuroscientist Dr Andrew D. Huberman points out in a 2022 podcast that dogs only have to be present in a room with you to reduce your anxiety and increase your happiness. Their effect on us is so strong that you don't even have to *know* the dog. Even patting a random one on the street can increase our feelings of wellbeing. Dog love is powerful; they are also much easier to come by than a human friend. You can simply go and get one from the SPCA or rescue shelter. Additionally, experiencing the unconditional love of this one being may ease the stress of loneliness enough that you feel confident to reach out to humans.

A study from 2023 entitled 'What is beneficial in our relationships with pets?' confirmed another thing that dog owners already know. They help you meet new people. Strangers are much more likely to come up and chat if you have a dog. They will mainly talk to your pooch, but you might get a connection on the side. Dogs are an antidote to loneliness. Their mere presence decreases feelings of isolation while helping us make more friends.

As I write this, my dog, Colin, is lying beside me on the couch. He is such a good boy. In a few moments I'll whisper 'Walk' in his ear and he'll go crazy. We will take a stroll round the block, he'll sniff things, we'll meet people, he'll have a big smile on his face, I'll have plastic bags for his disgusting leavings. We are best buds.

BURNING LOVE

In recent years I have put more effort into the relationships in my life. Whether it's saying a friendly hello to work-mates when you arrive at the office, learning a shopkeeper's name, being there for a buddy when they need you, or devoting your life to someone you love, human connection is the most important thing we do.

Right up there with eating. The interactions we have with our children, brothers, sisters, parents, friends, lovers and all the other humans we happen to encounter day to day, is the stuff a good life is made of.

With that in mind, I've been reaching out even when it's awkward, organising things for friends to do together and actually listening when they speak. If I found myself on fire in an ape suit today, I am confident that loneliness wouldn't be at the forefront of my mind. These days I would be much more focused on getting my burning arse out of the cage and into the extinguishing pool in the hope of remaining alive so I could spend as much time as possible with all the people I love.

A few weeks after the primate inferno, the person I was missing so much flew over to see me in London. A few years after that we had a child together and then another. That painful burning-monkey loneliness led to our lovely little family.

Well worth it.

Chapter Five

Offended?

It's 2006, and my band Deja Voodoo are playing shows to promote our second album, *Back in Brown*. In the two years since the release of our mildly successful debut *Brown Sabbath*, there's been a lot of restaurants, takeaways and pies in my life and absolutely no exercise.

It's the first night of tour and the band hits the stage pumped. The crowd goes wild. We bash out our opening number, 'We Are Deja Voodoo', and things are rocking. I sing well, I nail my solos and strike all kinds of cool poses. I'm feeling amazing. We finish the song with our guitars and drumsticks held above our heads in triumph. The crowd goes wild again.

A chant grows from up front. A row of ladies are yelling my name. This is great — I like people screaming for me. However, I can't quite hear all the words . . . so instead of starting the next song as planned, I lean my mic-stand out into the crowd. I want everyone to hear this sweet adulation loud and clear. But when it comes through the PA, it's not what I had hoped. 'Matt got fat,

Matt got fat, Matt got fat' blasts out across the venue. I quickly pull the mic back and pretend I didn't hear. Too late. The chant takes on a life of its own. 'Matt got fat, Matt got fat, Matt got fat.' Everyone from the front to the back of the pub joins in.

Who do they think they are? One song in to the first show of our triumphant return, and an entire audience is fat-shaming me. This is my band and my show — you don't chant 'Matt got fat, Matt got fat, Matt got fat' at me. It's hurting my feelings. I turn to the band for support, but all I get from them is three giant smiles; they could not be happier with the chant. Our lead guitarist joins in over his mic: 'Matt got fat, Matt got fat, Matt got fat.' The band has no plans to put me out of my misery by starting the next song. After 30 seconds — that feels like an hour — the crowd stops chanting and pauses for a second before spontaneously cracking up. They really enjoyed chanting 'Matt got fat' at me.

I have gone from pumped-up to full deflation in record time. I am offended. Not angry, not humiliated, not embarrassed; actually *offended*.

Then I make a huge mistake. I grab the mic and say the most uncool thing you could possibly say in such a situation: a snotty 'Okay, you've all had your fun. A real crack-up. Shall we play another song? That's what we're here for.'

The crowd boos.

* * *

Thanks to the devices in our pockets, communicating with others is easier than ever. As a result we have more opportunities to see and hear things we don't like. Having said that, taking offence is by no means a new thing. The Bible tells the tale of a bald man named Elisha being accosted by juveniles on his way to the ancient town of Bethel. They mocked his lack of hair, yelling, 'Go up, bald-head! Go up, bald-head!' Elisha cursed the kids in the name of YHWH, and the next day things took a shocking turn:

> . . . two female bears came out from the forest and mauled forty-two of those juveniles. —*Holy Bible: King James Version*, 2 Kings 2:23–24

Elisha was offended by the comments about his baldness, and YHWH appears to have taken his side on the matter and sent in the bloodthirsty she-bears. It's clear that people have been getting offended by the things others say for many thousands of years before the internet, phones and social media came along.

It's not good. Taking offence can affect your sense of self-worth and your mental wellbeing. It can lead to conflict or avoidance in relationships. We waste a lot of time and energy stewing on things we have deemed to be offensive. Feeling offended can also lead to self-censorship, where we refrain from expressing our true feelings or opinions for fear of being insulted further or of offending others. Discussion becomes shallow, dishonest or non-existent.

So what can we do about it?

As mentioned earlier, Stoic philosophy began in Greece around 300 BCE, before spreading to Rome. It's a thought system that focuses on resilience, virtue and rationality. The Stoics believed that we can control our internal responses to external events. Other people's opinions and words are external to us — what they say and think is up to them. We can't control that. We live in a world where people will say nasty things whether we like it or not.

The Stoics believed that we have the power to brush aside ridicule and disrespect and instead focus our energies in more positive directions. Allowing the whims of other people to upset us is a haphazard way to live. You are handing over your tranquillity and happiness to anyone who might come your way. That's giving away the only real power you have — the quality of your thoughts. Luckily, according to the Stoics, we don't *have* to be offended.

> Choose not to be harmed — and you won't feel harmed. Don't feel harmed — and you haven't been.
>
> —Marcus Aurelius, *Meditations*, p. 39

Understanding that I don't have to get upset when someone says something I don't like is one of the most helpful things I've learned in recent years. I can simply decide not to worry about it. A chant of 'Matt got fat' doesn't need to ruin my evening.

* * *

There are, of course, more challenging insults than the ones I experienced on stage. It was a long way from, for example, an intellectually disabled child being teased by bullies at school. On that stage I was in a reasonably strong position behind my guitar and mic. I am, as I said at the start of this book, completely unqualified to offer advice to people in tough situations. (In fact, I'm completely unqualified to offer advice, full stop.) I am, however, just smart enough to understand that the art of choosing not to be affected by other people's words and actions exists in degrees of difficulty. When people with major challenges in life rise above what other people think of them, they are achieving at a very high level.

Here, the British World War II patients of New Zealand-born plastic surgeon Archibald Hector McIndoe spring to mind. He treated RAF airmen with serious burns at the Queen Victoria Hospital in East Grinstead, England. Hurricane and Spitfire fighter planes carried a lot of fuel up-front and, as such, were prone to explode in the cockpit area during combat. When this happened, some of the unfortunate pilots were left with no features at all; their eyelids, noses, ears and lips all burnt off. Horrifying.

In treating these men, McIndoe not only made huge strides in plastic surgery, but also implemented some highly successful psychological innovations. He encouraged the burnt men in his care to integrate into society as soon as they possibly could.

McIndoe would take them to bars and social gatherings to get them used to the way people reacted to their injuries. He wanted them to choose to be proud of who they were, wherever they were, no matter how they looked to others or what people said. The men formed a social group called The Guinea Pig Club. They met up and celebrated each other and the work of McIndoe for the rest of their lives.

Many people finding themselves in that condition would have hidden away from the world, but most of these men went out and met new people, got married and had families. The footage of these badly disfigured pilots laughing and enjoying their time in public is inspiring; the Janson Media documentary *The Guinea Pig Club* is available on YouTube if you're interested.

Judging by the prissy way I behaved around a few people commenting on my weight, I doubt I would have had the mental toughness to embrace life the way these airmen did. People like me have to acknowledge that the things we face in life are in a different ball-park to the challenges of other people. Well, so far, anyway.

Having said that, and however hard it is to achieve, I believe it is in all of our best interests to control the negative emotions brought about by our interactions with the outside world. While no one will pull off this feat all of the time, life will be less punishing if we pull it off more often than not. It's an ideal to strive towards. One you will get better at with practice and the help of a few simple techniques.

* * *

To start with, when we feel insulted we might ask ourselves some questions about the perceived slight. Like:

Is it true? Can you be offended by what is real? If someone tells you that you smell bad and you *do* smell bad, is that an insult or simply an accurate description?

In the sixth century BCE, the Chinese Daoist sage Lao Tzu taught that it is more beneficial to accede to the demands of reality rather than protest against them. He believed that we must surrender to the universe.

Reality is a tough opponent — an ultimately unbeatable boss battle. Your bad smell already existed in the universe before it was pointed out. So if you take offence to that statement of fact, is that not just a failure to accept reality? You are not at peace with your universe.

In some cases, if we accept reality but don't like it, we can choose to take action. In the case of your stench you could accept that you stink and choose to do something about it. You could also accept that you stink, decide it's not important and continue as normal. Either way you are now at one with the truth and don't need to feel offended.

If the 'insulting' truth that has been pointed out is an unchangeable thing like your age, it is even more powerful to accept it and even more futile to hide from it. Take an insult like

'Shut up, old man', for example. You may choose to push back against the shutting-up part, but if you are old, you are old. We can't expect to go through life without people pointing out things that are true. Better to change your perspective around what is offensive to you. If you accept reality, then someone pointing it out shouldn't offend you.

You could instead choose to feel grateful for the info, no matter the manner in which the news is delivered or what the motive of the message is. You have been informed of something you didn't know; surely, gratitude would be a better response than taking offence. Newsflash: you smell bad. Great, you can use that information. I'd probably apply some underarm deodorant.

Conversely, if someone says you stink when you don't, then the comment has no meaning. It's nonsense and therefore is also not offensive. If someone claims in public that they can run faster than you and you know they can't, it would be silly to take offence. In that case, the person saying it has more reason to feel embarrassed than you.

My favourite Dutch philosophical YouTuber and author Einzelgänger describes the logic of this way of thinking in his excellent book *Unoffendable*.

> Insert insult. Is it true? If yes, then it is not an insult. Why be offended by it? If no, then it is nonsense. Why be triggered by nonsense? (p. 19)

Can I apply empathy? The Stoics believed that putting yourself in the shoes of your insulter can quell your personal hurt. If someone offends us, we can try to see things from their perspective. What did they hope to achieve? Why are they saying what they're saying? Why are they angry? You might feel some sympathy when you do that. You might recognise yourself in their behaviour; you may have said similar things in similar circumstances. Maybe they are envious of you. As mums have been pointing out forever: 'Don't worry about it: they're just jealous.' If this is true, have you been jealous of others? Marcus Aurelius puts it this way:

> Your sense of good and evil may be the same as theirs, or near it, in which case you have to excuse them.
> —in *Meditations*, p. 89

If we consider the perspectives, motivations and circumstances of the potential offender, it is much easier to respond with patience and compassion. You can turn offence into empathy.

How credible is the source of the insult? It's a sunny summer afternoon in 2014 and I am wandering up Auckland's Karangahape Road minding my own business on the way home from work. Suddenly, a large drunk man lurches out of a bar, takes a swing at me, misses and hits his hand on a post. He turns to me and screams, 'You broke my hand, you fucking asshole!' He tries to punch me again and misses a second time, mainly because I'm legging it down the road as fast as I can. The man yells further insults at me as I leave the scene: 'You fucking loser, you pussy, you're nothing.' While I am a little rattled by the encounter, I take absolutely no offence. This stranger doesn't know me well enough to pass judgement on my 'nothingness'. He doesn't seem like much of an expert in anything.

When deciding how much weight you will afford someone else's insult, it's a good idea to evaluate their competency. Ever since that K' Road incident, whenever I receive online abuse I bring that big drunk man to mind. Since I generally know nothing about the origins of the feedback, it might as well be a crazy drunk person taking wild swings.

Becoming upset by random opinions online is a risky business. Much of the internet is either fully or partially anonymous. For all you know, this person who is commentating, criticising, or sharing their thoughts with you online is insane, a joker, or an evil robot — or all three. Maybe it's an emotional seventeen-year-old who knows nothing about the world and has nothing to lose. Maybe it's a fourteen-year-old whose opinions aren't yet fully formed. Maybe it's a 55-year-old messing with you for fun. Most likely it's someone screaming into the void in the hope of getting a reaction.

If my dad tells me something about my health, I tend to take it on board. I know he's a good man who has my best interests at heart, and he is also smart and a doctor. His opinion is worth a lot to me. I would not take health advice from the drunk guy who tried to take my head off on K' Road, or from an anonymous person on the internet. They lack credibility.

So if you're about to take offence at the words or actions of another, it might be worth asking yourself if you even respect that person's opinion. As my good mate Manaia Stewart from the Alternative Commentary Collective says: 'Don't take insults from people you wouldn't take advice from.'

Do they mean it? There is always a chance that the words you are upset over have no meaning to the insulter. If they don't care about what they're saying, you would be silly to take it on board. Even if they care now, they might not later. It might be helpful to allow for the transient nature of opinions. What this person thinks now might not last a full sentence. People's opinions are often fleeting and may simply disappear with a change of mood.

In February 2011, on my first day as a commercial radio host, I was so nervous I nearly didn't make it into the studio; but I got through the first three-hour episode of *The Matt Heath Drive Show* on Radio Hauraki unscathed. That was until the very end, when a guy named Dave called me up and told me I was ruining the station and he wanted to kill me. He told me if I didn't quit he'd be waiting in the carpark for me with a 'fucking crowbar'. This call did not help my confidence. 'Death Threat Dave', as my co-host Tim Batt called him, threatened my existence twice in the next show. But then, at the end of our Wednesday edition, he rang up again to tell me he was wrong and he now loves the show. Death Threat Dave didn't want to kill me anymore. A huge turnaround in opinion from Death Threat Dave in a mere 48 hours.

It might also be worth considering that the person offending you is messing with you. Pushing your buttons. You can waste a lot of unnecessary energy trying to understand and respond to people who are being silly. The lead singer of the band Nirvana, Kurt Cobain, was a musical genius but a reasonably punishing guy to interview. People took the things he said very seriously when often he was just making stuff up for fun. In his personal journal Cobain wrote the following to himself, which was later published by *Newsweek*:

> I like to have strong opinions with nothing to back them up, besides my primal sincerity. I like sincerity. I lack sincerity. —quoted by Jon Wiederhorn, MTV.com

It might be helpful to remember that people don't always mean what they say.

Is it just an opinion? Recently, The Rewatchables podcast was discussing one of my favourite movies ever, *Raiders of the Lost Ark*. At one point, host Bill Simmons is arguing that the sadistic Gestapo agent Major Arnold Toht, played by Ronald Lacey, wasn't evil enough to be a scary villain, that it was merely his glasses, leather jacket and sweatiness that made him look evil. I am a huge fan of Bill Simmons, but to my surprise I found his opinion a little offensive. I stopped the pod to take a breath. Major Arnold Toht is a Nazi, and he was about to torture the lovely Marion with a red-hot poker in her Nepalese bar before Indy interrupted. I have been scared of Major Arnold Toht most of my life. How dare America's most successful sports and pop-culture podcaster make such a claim? Bill was questioning the validity of my childhood nightmares and it offended me.

That one difference of opinion made me turn off the pod. If I can feel put-out over something as vacuous as the scariness of a character in a movie, it's no wonder people struggle to have rational discussions about things that actually matter. The question of whether or not Major Arnold Toht is as scary as he should be is not something that can be boiled down to fact. Much of it is based on experience. I saw the movie for the first time as a small child, so this likely affects how scary I found the Nazi. My offence at Simmons's opinion is drenched in my own personal history with that movie.

Other people's opinions on politics, on sport, on art — or even on you — are theirs and not yours. We own our own opinions, and that's it. If you find yourself offended by what someone is saying, ask yourself: 'Is this just their opinion?' Marcus Aurelius was confounded by the weight we put on the thoughts of others:

We all love ourselves more than other people,
but care more about their opinion than our own.
—in *Meditations*, p. 162

Are you making it up? One of my favourite New Zealand writers, Diana Wichtel, recently reviewed a TV show I was appearing in. In her article she described me as 'radio host and surprisingly philosophical *NZ Herald* columnist Matt Heath'. In a weak moment I took this to mean 'Matt Heath, that complete idiot who is always spouting stupid philosophy in the paper'.

On reflection — I'm becoming increasingly wise to my own neurotic bullshit — I realised that this take was more likely a projection of my insecurities. To find out the truth, I hunted her down on social media. She told me it hadn't occurred to her that anyone could take a comment like that negatively. The point she was trying to make was this: Matt Heath's TV shows have generally been full-on. And on his radio show he once asked the prime minister if he does wees in the shower. Therefore, it was surprising for some to see him look deeper into the meaning of things in his *Herald* column.

In short, this was a compliment that I had attempted to turn into an insult.

Is the insult worth collecting? In sport, sledging is the practice of deliberately insulting or verbally intimidating an opposing player. The intention is to put your opponent off their game.

If, however, you choose to *enjoy* the sledge, then you take away its power. You can take this further and walk onto the field of play with the intention of collecting insults to share with others later. The very thing meant to annoy you becomes a precious resource to gather. You may even feel disappointed when you don't receive good ones.

We can use the same method in everyday life. If there is someone you have to deal with who likes to insult you, relish the words; enjoy them, rate them, share them with others. Collect them.

THE CASE FOR BEING OFFENSIVE

Most people try not to offend others if they can help it. On the surface, this seems like a nice way to behave: we don't want to walk around making people feel bad. But what if you come across a person who is making life difficult for themselves? To give yet another smelly example, what if they stink and they don't know? If you leave them in the dark about their odour for fear of offending them, they may get silently ostracised. I worked with one guy who stunk terribly. Horrible B.O. We all moved away from his area; no one said anything. After a while he left the job. He thought everyone hated him, when really we only hated his stench.

Niceness/cowardice might end up hurting the person more than any unfortunate truth or insult could. It might have been less hurtful to yell 'You freaking stink, mate' than to say absolutely nothing.

New Zealanders famously do not complain at restaurants and cafes. We get what we get, and we don't get upset. An advert on the Auckland radio station bFM in the early 2000s perfectly illustrated this attitude. A group of friends sit down for breakfast; things are going well until a man notices that there is an actual dog turd on his plate. The other people at the table are understandably outraged: 'You have to say something.' The man agrees — 'Yeah, I bloody will say something. It's a dog shit!' When the waiter returns to the table and asks 'How are your meals?', everyone, including the man who was served the turd, answers enthusiastically: 'Fine, thank you.'

Most business owners would prefer you to tell them that their food, products or services are bad, rather than go broke. Protecting people's feelings isn't always the nicest way to behave.

INSULTS — THE LANGUAGE OF LOVE

Banter between friends is a great demonstration of the subjective nature of offence. When we don't know each other very well, or there is a power difference such as boss and employee, or when meeting the parent of a new partner, we tend to adopt a polite, respectful style of communication. However, when we become close, intimate friends, we may start to demonstrate our love with insults. Max Dickins, who we met in Chapter Four, discusses this in his book *Billy No-Mates*. He points out that good male friends are brutal. The more they like each other, the more they insult each other. He believes that male aggression is counter-intuitively employed to achieve closer bonds. We can show love with insults. He writes that it is

> intimacy in action, communicating both 'I know you' and 'I know you trust that I'm not being cruel, that I have permission, that we are playing a game'. (p. 151)

You can say terrible things to someone when you know that they like you so much they won't hit you. From the point of view of the guy being hassled, the fact that this friend is saying this stuff means he must know how much you love him. He also knows you won't hit him. The more you test out that security, the stronger your bond.

We can speculate on the survival value of this behaviour from an evolutionary standpoint. It's likely a proof of toughness: if you can't endure good-natured teasing and aggression from your peers, you are unlikely to be able to handle a confrontation with a genuine enemy.

It's also a testing of wits. All my best friendships come with insults. Nothing makes us laugh more, or feel closer, than mean nicknames and using friends' most shameful moments as fodder. The joking is a way of saying: 'We love you for what you are.'

Obviously, the banter can go too far. If it's a show of mutual love through pushing things to the limit, that's one thing; but when someone is being a relentless, unfunny, mean arsehole, that's another. Good friends will have a different, more overtly caring side to their relationship, but when the nastiest thing someone can say to you makes you feel good, you know that person loves you.

* * *

If, after all this, you still choose to be offended, are you owed anything because of this? Should the fact that someone has (or says they have) had their feelings hurt end an argument? The great British comic and writer Stephen Fry addressed this issue in 2005. He told *The Guardian* newspaper that saying you are offended is

> actually nothing more than a whine. It has no meaning, it has no purpose, it has no reason to be respected as a phrase. 'I'm offended by that.' Well, so fucking what?
> —quoted in David Smith, 'I saw hate in a graveyard — Stephen Fry'

THANKS FOR THE ABUSE

If I found myself on stage now in front of a group of people yelling at me about my weight, I would behave differently. I wouldn't humiliate myself and invite the boos of the crowd by whingeing at them. I wouldn't allow the words of others to ruin an otherwise special experience.

The truth is, I *had* got fat. I'd been eating and drinking like a pig for over a year. Instead of feeling offended or sorry for myself, I could choose to feel grateful to the crowd for making my condition clear to me.

I might look to empathy, and ask myself when I had behaved in a similar way. The show we were making at the time, *Back of the Y*, had been described as the 'most offensive and abusive TV show ever made'. The lyrics to our song 'One Horse Town', which I wrote and would sing later in the show, go 'You fat fuck it'll all be over soon'. How could I be outraged at others for behaving the same way I had behaved so publicly myself? Instead I could collect the insult. A whole crowd chanting 'Matt got fat' is a fun story to share.

After that tour, I started a fitness regimen. I accepted that being overweight was bad for my health. That it was reducing the chances of me meeting my grandchildren. So I dropped 15 kilos. If I do live long enough to spend time with that next generation, I'll have those offensive young ladies in the front row to thank.

Chapter Six

Stressed?

It's Boxing Day, and my family and I have decided to go camping at a beautiful Northland beach holiday park. Me, the wonderful mother of my children, our two kids, and some extended family and friends. We plan to have a relaxing, stripped-back old-school vacation. It immediately becomes stressful. Things spiral dangerously out of control before we even leave the driveway.

I have been working solidly for the past week to finish several important projects. And I haven't got close. This weighs heavily on my mind, as does the fact that we need to be at the camping ground at 1 p.m. to meet some friends to let them in the gate.

These days, a camping trip involves an insane amount of gear, food and device-charging equipment. I put forward to the family the case for travelling light as our ancient ancestors did. As Yuval Noah Harari points out in his book *Sapiens: A brief history of humankind*, in our hunting and foraging days humans moved around with everything they owned on their backs. There were no wagons or even animals to help. As a result, they only carried the absolute essentials.

The idea is shot down, and instead I rise early to borrow a friend's massive brand-new van to transport several tonnes of stuff to the site. He isn't there, but he has left me instructions on how to get the key. I fail to understand these instructions and set off the alarm. It screams out across the early-morning suburban streets. Stress levels rise. I clench my fists.

We eventually get the van home; after an hour of inefficient, chaotic work, every millimetre of van space is crammed with essentials, including the huge tent I bought as a family Christmas present four years earlier. This monster cost me five grand and has only been erected once before.

Then, drama. Someone asks: 'Did you fill up the gas bottles for the cooker yesterday?' I had not, but for some reason I lie and say yes. Now I am really freaking out. We will starve up there with no fuel for the cooker and it's all my fault.

I sneak off to the service station, telling another lie about needing to pick something up. I forget my money card and can't pay for the gas. *Stress*. I go home, get the card, go back, get the bottles. Drop one on my foot getting it into the car. I sit behind the driving wheel for a few minutes, unable to pull out onto the road. My brain is overloading.

When I finally get back, the whole family jump in the front of the van. Things are going to be okay. And then . . . they aren't. The van doesn't start. It's less than a year old, but it won't go.

The starter motor spins but the engine won't catch. I put my head in my hands and whisper, dramatically, 'There is absolutely no fucking chance of us getting another van now and we need to leave *immediately*.' STRESS. I go to get my jumper cables from the boot of my car, but remember I lent them to someone else. I drive to their place to retrieve them. And they don't have them. Seconds later we find them in the back of the car I just drove over in. STRESS.

It's hard to line up the van and the batteries; I back into a feijoa tree trying. We connect the vehicles, fire up the cables, and — nothing. I scream, 'It's out of fucking gas!' 'But,' someone points out, 'you said you filled it up this morning.' Another lie has bitten me in the arse, my stress increases — again — and I head back to the service station in shame with a jerry-can in hand. Thirty minutes later we pour it in. And it doesn't do anything. STRESS. All I can think about is *the work I am not getting done*.

The clock is ticking; our friends will arrive at the holiday park soon. I slump to the ground, head in hands, and scream 'Fuck this!' Advice flies in every direction, from both young and old. Then my son clicks the remote, and the van starts. I had been using it as a physical key, meaning that the engine inhibitor hadn't been disarmed. Such a simple problem; why did it take so long to solve?

Because we have started so late, the traffic heading north is now atrocious. Our friends, who have been waiting an hour for us, now pile on the pressure with repeated text messages.

We arrive and it starts to rain. I check the WiFi at the campground and it's terrible. *When will I get to do my work?* STRESS! We find what I think is our camping spot and rapidly pull out the tent, but it's in a very different state than it was four years ago. It's now stinking, rotten and covered in black mould. No one should set foot in it, let alone sleep in it. STRESS! Erecting a tent is a pressure point for families at the best of times. When the thing is ruined and disgusting before you even start, you are in real trouble.

There are six of us and no other shelter available. How could a disaster like this happen? Who is to blame? Me. It's 100% my fault, so I get out the dishwashing brushes, get down on my knees, and literally rip the skin off my knuckles scrubbing. Muttering the whole time about work.

After an hour and a pint of spilt blood, the massive three-bedroom canvas tent is mould-free, pine-fresh and covered in my DNA. Time to put it up. Two and a half stressful hours later, we stand back as a family and admire what we have built. My son puts his arm around me: 'We made a little home.' I am too focused on the state of the WiFi to answer.

Then disaster strikes again. In my mad, stressed hurry I have pitched the tent in the wrong place. A camp official on a go-cart demands that we move, and that we do it right now.

It's getting dark. I pull at my hair. We knuckle down and begin the long task of packing up the whole campsite. The rain is now torrential. Our duvets, electronics, clothes, towels, food and board games are getting wet. STRESS! STRESS! STRESS! This camping trip has turned into a complete and utter unsalvageable disaster.

* * *

Why do small setbacks that you could easily deal with in isolation become unbearable when they occur close together? Why do we become stressed, flustered and panicky when we have lots of things to do? Why do we struggle to stay calm in the very situations we need to stay calm in?

It could have something to do with our limited capacity for real-time problem-solving. Professor of Psychology at the University of Missouri-Columbia Dr Nelson Cowan describes our different types of memory in an academic paper he wrote in 2014:

> Working memory is the small amount of information that can be held in mind and used in the execution of cognitive tasks, in contrast with long-term memory, the vast amount of information saved in one's life.
> —in 'Working memory underpins cognitive development, learning, and education', p. 197

Long-term memory can store huge amounts of information. It holds everything we are currently not using, and it can hold it for a very long time. Meanwhile, our working memory retains a small amount of information in a readily accessible form. We use it for problem-solving, planning, reasoning and comprehension on the fly. The relationship between the two types of memory is similar to the hard drive (long-term memory) and the RAM (working memory) in your computer.

In 1871, British economist and logician William Stanley Jevons wrote that

> . . . the mind is unable through the eye to estimate any large number of objects without counting them successively. A small number, for instance three or four, it can certainly comprehend and count by an instantaneous and apparently single act of mental attention. —in 'The power of numerical discrimination', p. 281

To prove this, Stanley conducted a series of wildly unscientific bean-based experiments on himself. Amazingly, though, he got it right. His finding — that human adults can deal with just three or four things at once — has since been replicated many times by modern scientists, including by Cowan in his 2001 paper 'The magical number 4 in short-term memory'.

Stressful situations take up slots in the tiny space of your working memory. If you're dealing with one problem and then another one arises, and then another, while you are dealing with other stuff, then things get stressful. To make matters worse, your worrying about what is happening takes up its own space in your working memory. Your systems get overloaded, and you lose your ability to deal with simple things. Your nervous system responds with panic. You become more and more stressed, and less and less effective.

This is likely where sayings like 'Take it one step at a time', 'Focus on the task at hand' and 'Just put one foot in front of the other' come from. Attack too many things at once, and we stress out and make mistakes.

* * *

Long-term stress promotes disease, affects your love-life, ruins your teeth and gums, damages your heart, creates wrinkles, destroys muscle, causes poor eyesight, weakens your immune system and can lead to long-term disability. But, like many of the things I talk about in this book, surely it has a purpose? I zoomed David Robson, science writer and author of *The Expectation Effect*, in London to ask him.

> **Me: If stressed people don't perform as well as calm people, if high blood pressure is bad and if hormones such as adrenaline and cortisol damage us over time, what good is stress?**

Dave: It's there to help you to deal with a challenge. When your heart is racing really quickly, it's pumping oxygen to your brain, which helps you to think more clearly. The hormones like cortisol, in the short term, elevate you. That physiological arousal is adaptive. They're actually sharpening your thinking and keeping you on the ball. You might feel a bit jittery before giving a talk or doing an exam. But it's better to feel a bit jittery than to feel sleepy. Research shows that if you get people to recognise the benefits stress is giving them, it actually improves their performance.

Me: So if you tell yourself those stressed feelings are helping, they do less damage?

Dave: Yes, you can take something that feels unpleasant, like stress, and remind yourself of the benefits it's bringing. If you are stressed, or nervous, your heart is racing, you are heating up. Remind yourself that that's your body providing the focus and resources you need to do what you need to do. It even helps you recover more quickly after the event. So the body goes back to this state called 'rest and digest'. Essentially, the cortisol levels are dropping back. If you have the negative view of stress, you're more likely to feel like you are suffering for longer. Maybe you hold on to it, continue it across the whole day. That's what leads to the long-term damage from stress.

So, stress is your body getting ready for what you need to face — but when we hold on to it, it starts to do damage. So it would seem wise to do what we need to do, finish it and then move on. However, a lot of the time stress doesn't come from the things we need to do, but from other things that are getting in the way of us doing them.

What can we do when life seems to be throwing multiple random stressful setbacks our way? In his book *The Stoic Challenge*, Professor William B. Irvine advises a reframing of these stressful events so that we see them individually. He believes we can look at setbacks as challenges to cheerfully direct our energies towards. We can pit ourselves against these stressful tests set for us by the universe and show our worth.

How do you react to a van that won't start when you're running late for a camping trip? If you lose your cool, slump to the ground with your head in your hands and scream 'Fuck this!', you have failed the test. But if you summon the energy that stress provides, get to work and solve the problem in front of you in an efficient and clever way, you have passed.

When you take on this mindset, you may even start to look forward to setbacks as ways to prove yourself. It can become a kind of sport. If you defeat a setback, and then another and another, all in an honourable, competent way, you earn that sweet joy of victory.

I zoomed Bill at his home in Dayton, Ohio, to discuss this.

Me: What should we do when stressful things just keep coming at us?

Bill: A lot of the damage setbacks do to us is self-inflicted; it is our frustration that hurts us most. If we calmly work around a setback, we can instead experience pride. That's where I bring in the Stoic gods. I don't believe the Stoic gods actually exist, but I act like they do. I imagine they're testing me. Not because they're mean, but because they care. A good coach pushes you, so you improve.

You can imagine there are Stoic gods who want you to be a tough human who can bounce back. So, when you have a setback, you can go: 'Okay, a test — what do I need to do to get to the other side of this?' You choose to take on that challenge and do what you need to do in a calm, brilliant way. You take pride in your response. This is true with small things like a flat tyre and the big things in life that will occur. You can look back and think, 'I met that challenge.' Everyone will experience hardship. Life will challenge you — are you up for the fight?

* * *

A week before I am due to travel overseas, I lose my credit card, driver's licence, work swipe-card, car-parking permit and a half-dozen other important things. My first instinct is to freak out, scream, yell and catastrophise. The trip is off; I have lost thousands of dollars and potentially my job. Then, remembering this idea of the challenge, I force myself to smile, take a breath, and view this as a test from the Stoic gods. Unfortunately, like Professor Irvine, I do not believe in them. For people who don't (which would be nearly everyone alive today), Irvine suggests that we imagine an earthly task-master. This person doesn't set the challenges for real and is unlikely to be there in person, but they must have your respect. Pick someone who makes a good imaginary coach.

I choose Willie Apiata. A former corporal in the New Zealand Special Air Service who received the Victoria Cross for bravery under fire after carrying a badly wounded comrade to safety across a deadly battlefield. Willie is considered our bravest soldier since the great Charlie Upham, who was awarded the Victoria Cross twice during World War II. Like Upham, Apiata is a humble man, who has donated his medals, mentors young people and doesn't trumpet his achievements, preferring to quietly help others where he can. Willie Apiata is the kind of guy you want challenging you and pushing you towards success. An excellent man to elevate to God status.

In this case it would appear that Willie has removed my wallet to test me. He has done this while I am up against a work deadline, have my flight coming up and am dealing with a sick child. This is one hell of a challenge. Willie and the universe are about to see exactly what I am made of.

The first thing I need is a new parking permit so my car won't get towed while I am overseas. Here, Willie places a sub-challenge in my way. The car is owned by my company, not me, so it's not registered to my house. 'No problem, Mr Apiata, whatever you need, sir.' I spend two hours online sorting out the most complex governmental bureaucratic nonsense you can imagine. When I near the end, Willie throws up another hurdle. I don't have a credit card to pay for the new licence, to get the registration change, to get the permit — because that was lost with the wallet. 'Very clever, Mr Apiata. This is a tricky one.' I will have to get a new credit card before I can continue.

One by one I face down Willie's challenges until I have a new wallet full of cards, a healthy kid back at school, my work completed and my arse on a plane.

Weeks later, and I still feel pride every time I pull a shiny new card from that wallet. But Willie gets me one last time. After arriving home from the trip, I lift the couch cushions that I was sure I had looked under, and there it is. Mr Apiata has returned the original wallet. It was never missing in the first place.

Taking a breath and refusing to get annoyed about all that wasted time replacing a wallet that was never really lost is the biggest challenge of all. It's a brilliant post-mission test from Mr Apiata. I fail that one, but overall I receive a solid B+ from the universe.

* * *

When we become stressed, the more recently developed parts of our brains become overloaded and the primitive parts take over. With our reasoning offline, knee-jerk fears bubble up from the depths of our mind and stand there unchallenged. We may start to catastrophise. The more stress there is, the stronger the primitive brain gets and the more threatened we feel. If you're running late, you become sure you will lose your job over it. If you've said something stupid, you're convinced everyone hates you. If you've failed to fill the gas canisters for a camping trip, you assume that no one will be able to eat and the family will go hungry.

It's hard to get things done with worst-case scenarios whizzing around your brain. Dr Amy Arnsten, a professor of neuroscience at Yale School of Medicine and co-author of the paper 'This is your brain in meltdown', offers advice for individuals overwhelmed by stress. She suggests you find something easily achievable that you know you can do, and then do that small thing. Success, no matter how minor, can help our prefrontal cortex take charge again and shut down the catastrophising. It could be something as simple as successfully taking a shower, changing your clothes, or just picking things up and putting them down again. Anything you can definitely succeed at. This can trick your brain into thinking you have brought things under control and it no longer needs to run in full stress mode. Research suggests that this method is particularly effective if the easy victory you choose helps others. Making sandwiches or cups of coffee will do it. These are wins that can reset your stress and get you thinking rationally again.

* * *

A 2021 study at Stanford Medicine, co-led by neuroscientist and podcaster Andrew D. Huberman, looked into a pattern of breathing that might bring rapid reductions in stress levels. They wanted to find a technique that people could use in day-to-day life, wherever and whenever stress appeared. There are many tools out there to combat stress: meditation, nutrition, good social connections, retreats, and a drink with friends. As effective as these are, they take time. You have to step away from the activity that's stressing you out.

Research led Huberman's team to a type of breathing called the 'physiological sigh', which was first discovered in the 1930s. It's a double inhale plus an exhale that works to reduce high levels of carbon dioxide in the bloodstream. We sometimes do it automatically when we're sleeping. Your dog probably does it often, too. Huberman and friends found that purposely performing the 'physiological sigh' lowers stress rapidly. As he describes in his YouTube video:

> It's a double inhale, and typically the first inhale is longer than the second, but the second one is still important to do, and then a very long, extended exhale.

Your lungs are made up of millions of little sacs. If laid out flat they would cover the surface of a tennis court. These sacs facilitate the intake of oxygen, but also the offloading of carbon dioxide. The second inhalation at the end of the first long one makes sure that all the sacs that might have been deflated are full. So you expel more carbon dioxide when you breathe out. The rapid offloading of all this carbon dioxide lowers stress.

So if things are ramping up, you're stressing and it's all getting out of control, take a moment. Breathe in through your nose until you've comfortably filled your lungs. Then take a second, deeper inhale of air to expand your lungs as much as possible. Then, exhale through your mouth until all the air is gone. Two or three of these 'physiological sighs' in a row is all you need to bring your level of stress down and allow you to calmly face the challenge in front of you.

I do this kind of breathing even when I'm not stressed. I enjoy a few inhales and exhales while driving to work, in a lift, or walking to a meeting. You might be surprised how good it makes you feel.

* * *

Telling lies is an excellent way to complicate life and pile on stress — whether it's making untrue statements, creating false or misleading impressions, hiding secrets or telling white lies. In his book *Lying*, neuroscientist Sam Harris makes a strong case against dishonesty. He points out that a liar must expend mental space and energy to uphold a falsehood, remembering what he has said to whom and when. This is effort you could be using for authentic communication. The stress grows because the liar then has to analyse every conversation to protect the lie. Whether you get rumbled or not, it generally makes things more complex and difficult.

Sometimes, untruths appear to further our careers, get us out of scrapes and help people in need. More often, though, they create entanglements that we struggle to escape. Yet we all tell lies to varying levels. Try going for a whole day without telling any untruths at all; not even a complimentary white lie. It's surprisingly hard. The first day I attempted to stop lying, I got up at 5.30 a.m. and had failed by 5.32 a.m. when I told the first person I spoke to that I liked her new matching shirt-and-shorts outfit. It might be beyond us to give up lying completely, but over time our lives become more straightforward and simple the less of it we do.

Dishonesty does more than just cause stress; it undermines who we are, damages the people around us, and ultimately makes the world a worse place. I have been dishonest many times in my life. It has brought stress to myself and to many others. At ten years old, I tell a friend's mother that I live in the large mansion down the road. A few months later, we organise a play date. She drops her son off at the flash house; he knocks on the door, but of course they don't know who he is. Confused, he walks off down the street and gets lost, and two families end up searching for him for hours. When we find him he is sitting in a park, cold, alone and very upset. So much unnecessary stress over a dumb lie, told purely because I wanted someone's mother to think I was richer than I am. Pathetic.

Self-aggrandising lies have to be among the most embarrassing when rumbled. These are the type of untruths we adults are prone to tell when we've been drinking. Exaggerating what you earn, claiming connections with people that you don't have, or lying about romantic activities are never things to feel proud of. They create all kinds of stress.

Even seemingly harmless lies create chaos. You are running late. You message the person waiting and tell them you will be there in five minutes, when you know it will take 30. It feels like you've released stress in the moment, but you haven't. That next 30 minutes of struggling to get to the meeting are all the more stressful for the lie. You are fighting against reality. On arrival, you will likely add another lie to explain the missing time. One that could be rumbled at any moment. 'Sorry, the traffic on the bridge was terrible.' 'Really? I was just talking to Mum. She was on the bridge, told me it was free-flowing.'

It's nearly always better to take the hit and tell the truth. Say to the person waiting: 'I am going to be half an hour late. Sorry. Totally my fault.' The truth is a real stress-reliever. Bold and a little painful at the time, but much less complex in the medium and long term.

STRESS CAMPING REVISITED

After the tent is up — clean and in its right place — we make dinner and I can finally do the work I have been stressing about all day. I rush off towards the WiFi area at the campground, but trip on a tent peg and send my laptop flying into a puddle. I dive for it, desperately pulling it out of the water. It's drenched. Likely ruined. I lie face-down on the ground for a moment, unable to move. The stress is coursing through my veins. I literally yell 'Why me?' and bang my head on the ground.

Then it strikes me: 'Fuck it.' I get up, walk back to the family, sit down on a camp chair and look around at the beautiful scenery. I smile, and the stress disappears. It leaves me so quickly when I let it go. It's almost as if it was of my own creation.

There's no doubt that prior to this moment the reasoning part of my brain had shut down and thrown me into full primitive stress mode. The mistakes piled up. Bad decisions were made. Catastrophising took over.

The rational brain, if it had been in charge, would have informed me that the family were never going to go hungry without gas, to follow the alarm instructions and to read the campground map before pitching the tent.

When faced with a similar day in the future, I plan to lean in to the challenges, framing every complication as a test to be confronted head-on. If a tent comes out of its bag mouldy, I'll smile to myself and think: 'Very clever, Willie Apiata, very clever.'

Then I'll face the challenge calmly and honourably. If asked whether I have filled the gas bottles when I haven't, I will tell the truth, apologise and get it done. When things get out of hand, I'll earn myself a stress-relieving win by making everyone a drink. When the van won't start, an alarm goes off, or a thousand text messages from impatient co-campers come through, I will take in two quick breaths and follow those with a long exhale.

When all the challenges have been met and I am sitting with the ones I love, out in nature, drinking warm beer out of dirty plastic cups, pride will be the appropriate earned emotion.

Chapter Seven

Humiliated?

Leslie, a reasonably good-looking man in his mid-twenties, has been with his girlfriend Laura for a few years. The pair are deeply in love and plan to travel to her family home in the English countryside so that Les can impress her father in the hope of getting his approval for their marriage. Les buys Laura's father an expensive bottle of whisky, two of port and some fancy bubbles for her mum. A train ride, a curry and two Cornish pasties later, the couple arrive at Laura's parents' large rural home. Les and Laura are tired but confident that a good impression can be made before bedtime.

Laura's mum, dad, older sister, brother and a grandparent have assembled for a formal welcoming dinner. Things go well . . . at first. Les is charming and engaging and, despite his large food intake over the past few days, manages to consume three servings of Laura's mum's famous fish pie. Feeling good about how things are going, the young suitor celebrates with a glass of red, then another and another, and then a white. After a port, the whisky comes out. A heavily inebriated Les throws caution to the wind, puts his arm around Laura's dad's shoulder and suggests they get up early to watch a game of rugby on TV. He's thinking that once he gets Dad alone he can ask for Laura's hand. After some encouragement from mother and daughter, the father reluctantly agrees to the early-morning viewing and Les heads off to bed in a separate room from Laura.

Keen to get a good sleep so he can continue making a good impression, the hopeful Kiwi pops two sleeping pills and he's out in seconds.

Early the next morning, Laura's dad sits on his newly imported Boca do Lobo couch waiting for Les. You could not find a classier place to watch sport with your father-in-law-to-be. It's the perfect setting to ask for a daughter's hand in marriage. But something strange has happened. A powerful combination of booze, Cornish pasties, fish pie and sleeping pills has rendered Les disorientated. The door swings open, and he shuffles into the lounge with a distant look in his eye.

The dad greets him, but there is no response from his potential son-in-law. Instead, Les lifts the couch cushion with purpose, turns, pulls down his pants and sits like he's in a bathroom. Then the unthinkable happens. Les unleashes the previous 24-hour feeding frenzy into the soft underbelly of the family sofa. Dad screams, Mum runs in. She also screams. Les is completely oblivious. He takes his time to get it all out, then calmly stands up, puts the couch cushion back down and shuffles back out the door, happy with a job well done. He returns to bed unaware of the heinous, public crime he has committed into a $15,000 couch.

A few hours later, Les rises to find a tense breakfast table waiting for him. Dad doesn't look up; Mum has turned green, and Laura's sister and brother sport strange smirks. Les greets them politely and sits down, grabbing himself a piece of toast from the rack. As he carefully butters it, making sure to watch his table manners, he enquires, 'Is everything okay?' A silence fills the room. Then the love of his life, Laura — the woman he would do anything to impress — bursts out laughing: 'You took a shit in the couch, right beside Dad. You fucking idiot.'

* * *

Humiliation is a member of the shame family of emotions, along with guilt and embarrassment. It can be painful and isolating. A loss of face may cause us to withdraw from others. But dealt with in the right way, it can be useful.

We evolved the feeling of humiliation as a behavioural motivator to help us navigate our status within groups. As deeply cooperative creatures, shame is an emotional warning that our social standing has been affected. In his book *Shame: Free yourself, find joy, and build true self-esteem*, American clinical psychologist Dr Joseph Burgo explains that our sense of shame evolved when humans lived in small groups and tribes. If you stepped out of line, violated social codes or acted in a way that risked the tribe, you found yourself shunned, isolated and unprotected from the world. According to American psychologist Silvan Tomkins, shame was so crucial to our survival that it's encoded in our DNA. He describes it as an 'inherently punishing' emotion — it certainly feels that way when the blood rushes to your face after someone rejects you.

Nowadays, humiliation comes in many flavours. We feel it when we say the wrong things in the office, wear the wrong outfits to functions, when we're insulted, rejected, diminished or demoted. We torture ourselves over our status within any group we happen to be in as if our lives still depended on it. Often it doesn't end with the embarrassing act: we will hurt ourselves again and again by ruminating on that stupid thing we did. 'She must think I'm an absolute loser', 'Why did I say that to that dude?', 'Why am I such a cock?'

On the website Psychology Today, British psychiatrist Neel Burton discusses the claims everyone makes about their status. Some claim to be leaders. Other claims are more modest, like being competent at a job or having a happy relationship. When we are embarrassed, these status claims come into question but we can bounce back. However, when we get completely humiliated it's not as easy to recover. If the shame is bad enough, our status collapses and we no longer feel we are worthy to make any claims about ourselves at all. It would be safe to say Les's claim that he was a good marital prospect for Laura was called into question when he confused the family couch with a bathroom.

Interestingly, much of the shame we modern humans experience is associated with bodily functions and nudity. In *Shame*, Dr Joseph Burgo points out that while our ancestors urinated, defecated and had sex in full view of others, today we do everything we can to keep these bodily functions invisible. As we became more and more civilised, shame drove those activities into hiding. Nowadays, nearly everyone would feel shame if someone walked in on them on the toilet. This feeling of shame about our basic functions is one of the tenets of civilisation.

Les not only failed to live up to his claims about himself, he also fell below what is expected of a modern human. Les's confused act was a rejection of society at a time when he was aiming to prove how civilised he was. As such, the humiliation was particularly intense. The fact that he wasn't in control at the time doesn't get him off the hook; he chose to eat and drink far more than he should have. That is part of the shame: 'Why did I get so steamed?'

* * *

While Les actively humiliated himself, we can of course get humiliated by others, too. For example, the Brazilian football team got well and truly humiliated by Germany in the final of the 2014 FIFA World Cup. The 7–1 thumping was particularly embarrassing because of Brazil's reputation as the best football team in the world, the ease with which the Germans scored goal after goal, and the fact that the tournament was being held in Brazil in front of a home crowd.

An excellent example of historical self-humiliation was the Battle of Karánsebes in Eastern Europe. On the evening of 21 September 1778, some light cavalry from the 100,000-strong Austrian force were sent out to look for signs of the Ottoman army in the area. They didn't find any trace of the enemy, but they did find some Romanians selling schnapps and they got stuck in. When another group of Austrian soldiers saw the drunken party, they headed over and demanded some booze. The first group didn't want to share and a fight broke out; shots were fired and several spooked, drunken Austrian horsemen galloped back to base camp yelling and screaming. Soldiers guarding the entrance confused the inebriated yelling for Turkish war cries. Assuming they were under attack by the Ottomans, they opened fire on their own men. Panic swept through the camp; the alarm was raised and sleeping soldiers jumped out of bed to join the fight against their own forces. It quickly turned into a full-scale battle and a blood-bath — with no one but the Austrian army present. Some historians claim casualties reached as high as 10,000. The skirmish has become known as the 'dumbest battle ever' and one of the worst self-inflicted humiliations in history. The surviving commanders lived with the shame of that defeat for the rest of their careers.

Of course, there are people who suffer deep shame in their

lives brought on by terrible treatment in childhood, sexual abuse, disability, or severe body dysmorphia. While I have nothing but sympathy for such people, this book isn't able to help with that; professional therapy might be the best course of action there. This chapter is focused on self-inflicted humiliations at a personal level; the meat-and-veg shame that plagues people who are otherwise okay. Shame that loses us status at work and in our social groups. The kind that makes us question whether we like ourselves when we're trying to get back to sleep at three in the morning. The kind I have often woken to after a big night out.

* * *

According to the Stoics (the ancient Greek and Roman philosophers I bang on about constantly in this book), we all have a set of behaviours that fit our natures. In *The Moral Landscape: How science can determine human values*, neuroscientist Sam Harris argues that these human values are facts that can be understood scientifically. C.S. Lewis talks about a 'law of nature' in his book *Mere Christianity*. He claims that there is a standard of good and decent behaviour that is obvious to everyone, and that this innate feeling of right and wrong is a clue to the meaning of the universe. Marcus Aurelius held a simplistic but similar view:

> If it's not right, don't do it. If it's not true, don't say it.
> —in *Meditations*, p. 177

We experience humiliation when we violate the behavioural expectations we have of ourselves. We know how we want to behave, and we don't like ourselves when we display more dishonesty, drunkenness, laziness, gluttony, anger, cruelty or cowardice than we expect of ourselves. As Marcus wrote:

> Shame is an emotion that we feel when we believe
> we are not living up to our own standards.
> —in *Meditations*, p. 130

Shame is an inevitable and painful part of being human, so what can we do about it when it happens?

DEALING WITH HUMILIATION

Most of us have a voice inside our head that yabbers away. It goes particularly hard at us when we are experiencing shame and humiliation. There's a 1990 study by Rodney Korba that claims our internal chatter can run at 4000 words per minute. That's a lot to deal with in a weakened state.

Internal chatter evolved to help us evaluate our past and prepare for the future, but often it just goes on and on and doesn't solve anything. It *can* motivate and coach us, but often it just stresses us out. Unchecked, a loop of negative self-talk can sap the neurons needed for our executive functions. When that happens, we struggle to do anything positive. Luckily, there are techniques we can use to gain perspective in shameful moments.

I zoomed Ethan Kross, American experimental psychologist, neuroscientist, writer and the world's leading expert on controlling the conscious mind. This man has spent much of his life formulating mental tools to deal with our internal monologue. I asked Ethan what we can do with our inner voice when we find ourselves humiliated. He told me:

> You can give yourself advice as a friend might. Using your own name can be useful for shifting your perspective. We know from lots of research that we find it easier to give good advice to others than to ourselves. It can help to say something like: 'Ethan, calm down; this is not the end of the world.'
>
> Another tool I find really useful in the heat of the moment is to remind myself how I'm going to feel about this thing tomorrow or next week, or next year. There's a lot of science behind this. We call it 'temporal distancing'. When you are zoned in and spinning your wheels, it feels like this issue you're experiencing is all-consuming. What we lose sight of is the fact we've experienced these emotional ups and downs throughout our lives. And guess what? They tend to normalise over time. Simply remind yourself that you're probably going to feel better about this thing you have done tomorrow, and if not tomorrow, next week or next month.

You can also mix those two tools. When you wake up in the middle of the night ruminating on something, try asking: 'Ethan, how are you going to feel about this in the morning?' The quickest way to turn down chatter is to get some distance.

* * *

When you're mired in rumination, it might be helpful to note that you care about what happened more than anyone else does. We grossly overestimate how much people notice, care, or even think about us. Often, when we feel shame, we are the only ones who are across the situation in any detail. In psychology, this is what's known as the 'spotlight effect'. We are the centre of our lives; the things we do and say are everything to us. Being aware of the spotlight effect lets us recognise that everyone else is also mainly thinking about themselves.

Thomas Gilovich and colleagues tested this phenomenon in a 2002 paper published in the *Journal of Personality and Social Psychology*. The researchers invited groups of students to work together on an unrelated task. In each group, one of the participants was randomly assigned an embarrassing T-shirt featuring a large image of American singer Barry Manilow. Apparently, Southern California hipsters at the time thought this a deeply shameful item of clothing. The student wearing the embarrassing T-shirt was then asked to estimate how many people in the room would remember what was on it. Across the trial, the wearers estimated that around 50% would notice; it turned out to be less than 20%. In other words, when you feel embarrassed about something, you think others care much more than they do.

In their next study, the researchers focused on embarrassing utterances. Once again, the students drastically overestimated how many people would notice what they'd said.

This lack of interest is a problem if you're trying to make an impact, but can be a source of comfort when ruminating on a perceived humiliation in your life. There is a very good chance that you are the only one thinking about what you did or said. That idiotic joke that no one laughed at, your drunken dancing, your failed attempt at charming a person you fancy, your fly being open, the red wine stain on your shirt, the fall you took, the job you lost. No one cares as much as you do. If humiliation as an emotion exists to warn us of a loss of social status, then we haven't lost much if no one else noticed. How much time we waste lying awake, hassling ourselves, when our humiliation has been forgotten by everyone but us — if they were even aware of what happened in the first place?

* * *

Comparison is another way to gain distance from your chatter. Most of us will go through our whole lives and never reach

Les's couch-soiling level of humiliation. The next time you do something you are not proud of, compare your shame with his, or with someone you know who has done worse. It's an easy way to gain perspective. Put next to Les's trip to his girlfriend's parents' lounge, your embarrassment over a failed joke will wither and die. The humiliation you feel over a declined credit card in front of friends will not stand up against the heat of his fantasy bathroom experience.

Whatever you have done, you will most likely know friends who have done something similar — or worse. Ask yourself if you still like them. Do you think substantially less of them? If you can forgive your friend, they will likely forgive you for your indiscretion, and you can forgive yourself.

Feeling embarrassed over the reactions of a few people may seem less important when you look at famous humiliations like the ones outlined in Jon Ronson's 2015 book *So You've Been Publicly Shamed*. Take Justine Sacco, a PR executive who tweeted a joke about AIDS in Africa just before taking off on a flight. By the time she landed and turned on her phone again, her career was over. She faced a brutal bombardment of criticism, abuse and death threats from around the world. In her own words, she felt 'deeply humiliated, ashamed and embarrassed'. This was shaming on a global scale. Compare that against your tripping over and spilling coffee on a single person, and you might not feel so bad.

If a global perspective doesn't help, a universal one might. In his book *Four Thousand Weeks: Time management for mortals*,

Oliver Burkeman offers the largest possible perspective available. He talks of the counter-intuitive comfort we can get in times of trouble by acknowledging the meaninglessness of our existence against the backdrop of an uncaring universe — a technique called Cosmic Insignificance Therapy. I zoomed him at his English home in August 2022 to discuss.

> **Me: How can focusing on our insignificance make us feel better?**

> Oliver: Putting your life in perspective lowers the stakes very quickly. The universe is vast and uncaring; you occupy a very small part of it for a very small length of time. If you acknowledge that in 200 years, nobody will care about anything you ever did, then why not just do it.

Your loss of social status isn't a billionth of a billionth of a drop of *anything* in the big scheme of things. Not only will it be forgotten, but so will you, as well as everyone who could judge you. So if you are feeling embarrassed because you brought the wrong bottle of wine to a party, maybe give yourself a break. It doesn't matter. If you are scared to make that speech at work, it might be helpful to note that all the biggest, most embarrassing things humans have ever done will one day mean absolutely nothing. It's an empowering idea. Why waste the precious seconds you have on Earth feeling shame over insignificant things?

OWNING THE NARRATIVE

I have a friend who got steamed on a UK work trip in the early 2000s and ended up making love to the bus driver against a back tyre. Their timing was poor, as everyone arrived back mid-act. She wasn't rostered on the next day, but came into work anyway. Just before lunch, she stood up in the middle of the shop, got everyone's attention, and yelled, 'You all saw what I did — that was weird and humiliating. I feel like an idiot. Can everyone please laugh at me now and get it over with? Say what you have to say while I am here. To my face, so I don't hate myself all weekend.'

She changed the story from 'Alannah made love to that gross bus driver on the side of the road' to 'What a legendary way to deal with the situation'. She owned the narrative.

In 2019 my animation company won Best Children's Television Programme at the NZTV Awards for our show *Welcome to Cardboard City*. I over-celebrated and turned the victory into a loss. At the after-party, I punished New Zealand's most-loved broadcaster Hilary Barry and her husband for far too long with the same unfunny joke. Then I stayed up all night and went live on my radio show the next morning.

The broadcast turned into three offensive, profanity-filled hours of me drunkenly yelling, 'You drink what I give you boy, you get it in you boy, you drink what I give you boy' at my co-host Jeremy Wells. It's one thing to say stupid stuff at a pub to your friends; quite another to do it in front of hundreds of thousands of listeners. There's a whole extra level of anxiety and self-hatred created when you know that everything you said is out there and recorded. My boss stood me down from commentating a game of cricket that day. He was trying to save me from further embarrassment, but in my drunken state and to my great shame, I took his actions as an affront to my professionalism. I fired him a bunch of long, passive-aggressive text messages from a bar on Auckland's beautiful waterfront, before throwing half a chicken across the table at a friend for a laugh.

Somehow I made it home, and slept for ten hours before waking up so embarrassed that I wasn't sure I'd ever leave my room again. Wallowing in self-pity and shame, I constructed a plan. I would control the narrative. First I delivered a heartfelt apology to my boss, then booked an interview with Hilary Barry on my radio show to discuss my behaviour at the awards. Next I wrote a tell-all article in the *Herald*, and finally I gave up alcohol for six months and started running five kilometres a day.

The experience was humbling. There was no excuse for my behaviour. But instead of pretending it didn't happen, or trying to play it down, leaning in to my behaviour helped. If you tell the story on your own terms, the humiliation loses its power. If you own it, control it and learn from it, you can create some distance from it. You become someone who is in a position to forgive yourself. As the cheesy saying goes: 'If you own it, you can give it away.'

This method is particularly powerful when humour is involved. Laughter and shame have an interesting relationship: if others laugh at you, you may feel shame; but if you find humour in your embarrassing situation, the humiliation shrinks away. Psychiatrist and shame researcher Michael Lewis believes that laughter is physiologically antagonistic to shame. Laughing at what we have done puts us in the position of an observer and, as such, dissociates us from the event.

George Michael's appearance on Michael Parkinson's interview show in 1998 is one of the best examples you will find of someone employing humour and 'owning' a humiliation. George had recently been arrested in Beverly Hills, California, for performing a 'lewd act' in a public bathroom. Right from the first few words on the show, his self-deprecating humour had the audience in stitches. He started by saying how much his mum respected Parkinson and how as a boy it was the only show he was allowed to stay up late to watch. He said he felt privileged to be there because of his mum's love of the show, but added that she might not be so thrilled that he had to get his willy out in public in order to get on. Later that year George released the global hit single 'Outside' making fun of the incident, which rejuvenated his career. Things didn't turn out great for the man — he went to jail in 2010 after crashing his Range Rover while wasted and then passed away in 2017 — but in 1998 he turned a potential humiliation into a victory by owning the narrative.

MAKING PLANS

According to the Stoics we must accept our humiliation, learn from it and move on. Rather than denying or suppressing it, we should welcome it, focus on its causes, resolve to make change and then stop hassling ourselves about it.

Say you turn up unprepared for a crucial day at work. You let everyone down and humiliate yourself by not being able to do what needs to be done. In this case, you would use your shame as a springboard, decide never to be underprepared again and make plans to ensure that this becomes a reality. Put more simply, if you feel embarrassed because your fly was down during a presentation, you could resolve in future to check your zipper before you walk up. Acknowledge the reason for your humiliation, and use it to better yourself — turning a current negative into a positive.

Dr Joseph Burgo believes that pride is gained when we achieve our goals, and shame when we fall short. We don't like to share our failures with others, and as a result shame can push us towards social isolation. Conversely, we tend to enjoy sharing our successes. When we have achieved something through planning and hard work and have done it in a way that makes us respect ourselves, it draws us closer to other people. In this way, achieving goals is the opposite of shame. It builds self-worth and connection. When the people we love and respect acknowledge our success, it is all the more sweet.

A humiliation that sets us off on a journey towards one of these pride-inducing goals can be seen as a blessing. We can transform humiliation into dignity. As Joseph Burgo writes:

> We need to listen to, and learn from, shame so we may eventually earn self-respect. —in *Shame*, p. 46

LIFE AFTER THE COUCH

Les used his living-room bathroom visit to motivate major change in his life. He realised that he had a wider drinking problem, and cut back. He got healthy, and these days he eats well, too. Les tells his disgusting story often, sharing it with anyone who will listen. He owns it and feels comfortable talking about it because he learned from his shame so that he can feel pride in where he is now.

Les hasn't soiled a couch in months.

Chapter Eight

Greedy?

> We humans are unhappy in large part because we are insatiable; after working hard to get what we want, we routinely lose interest in the object of our desire. Rather than feeling satisfied, we feel a bit bored, and in response to this boredom, we go on to form new, even grander desires. —Professor William B. Irvine, Zoom interview, 9 April 2022

It's 2017, and our little family is pretty happy with our car. She's doing everything we need her to do. Plenty of room for Mum, Dad, two kids and a pile of stinky sports gear in the back. Then, from the depths of my mind a powerful desire appears. We suddenly need a new 4x4 and we need it *stat*. What ignited this lust, I do not know. It may have been an advert, a conversation, or the sight of one of these beautiful models driving by. Wherever it came from, the idea spreads and soon all we can talk about is getting this new vehicle.

There is a fancy 4x4-sized hole in our hearts that needs to be filled. All conversation turns towards the justification of such an expense. The new vehicle would be great for taking stuff to the dump, camping, skiing, the kids' sports. Our current car is more than capable of all these things, but we 'need' a brand-new, bigger one. It has parking cameras in all directions, a huge engine and leather seats. We start driving by car-lots to ogle the beast. We become excited when the car appears on TV. One March morning we take the plunge and purchase the object of our desires, and what a thing of beauty our new ute turns out to be. The smell, the sound of the engine, its sheer size in the showroom. Oh, the elation as we drive our new truck, with all the extras, out of the dealership.

The kids are equally stoked when we surprise them at school pick-up. In this moment we all know for sure that our lives have changed. Adventure awaits. We have found happiness.

Then, out of the blue, it doesn't make anything better. I drive to work feeling much the same as I did before. Then the doubts start to creep in. Why did we pay so much for a massive four-wheel-drive when we work in offices and live in central Auckland? A week in to owning the beast, my son leaves the back door open while I'm reversing out of the driveway. It bends off and has to be replaced. My beautiful vehicle, ruined before the new-car smell has faded. Then, jealousy kicks in. My friend Pete buys a flasher one. Our car is a month old and already feels a bit lame. To fix that, I decide we need — mags! They don't help. Two years later my lovely new car is a scratched-up, rotting-junk-food-filled, unloved shell of its former glory. Much like myself. Basement levels of dissatisfaction have returned.

Maybe I can fill the gap in my heart with another new car? We talk ourselves into it. It feels great driving it out of the dealership — then a week later I feel nothing again. Maybe descending more deeply into debt to get an even flasher one will fill this new hole?

* * *

Humans have evolved from simple organisms with simple motivations. In the name of survival, we were compelled to wiggle our little tails to propel ourselves through the water towards advantageous things like food and away from dangerous things like predators. While there are many more variables running through our incredibly complex modern brains, the basic principles remain and, as outlined in Chapter Two, dopamine is heavily involved.

Remember, dopamine is, essentially, a motivator of action. We seek out behaviours that release dopamine, and in the process learn to repeat those actions. However, in complex beings like modern humans, dopamine isn't just released when we get what we want — it's also released in anticipation. A desire pops into our heads, often from the primitive parts of our brains; this generates a dopamine peak and the desire takes form. Soon afterwards, our dopamine levels dip from that peak to below baseline levels. They will stay that way until we get that object we desire. We are not really craving the object — we are craving the hit that we will get from acquiring it.

Budgets, debt and common sense are all useless in the face of such desires because logic isn't the point. Once our sights are set, we will overspend, borrow, do whatever we can to earn that hit. And of course it doesn't last; it wouldn't be doing its job if it did.

We are always wanting: when we get what we desire, our dopamine returns to baseline levels or below, and we begin to want either more of the same or something else, often both. This is why getting is more fun than having. Most of us are destined to repeat this cycle over and over again, partly because we are unaware that it exists. We assume we want things because we need them. Nope. We want them because we want *dopamine*. We want things simply because we are wired to want more things. More often than not, we end up spending resources, energy and time chasing things that give us nothing more than more wants in return.

* * *

In 1971, Canadian and American psychologists Philip Brickman and Donald T. Campbell wrote a paper called 'Hedonic relativism and planning the good society'. In it they coined the phrase 'hedonic adaptation'. This theory posits that people repeatedly return to their baseline level of happiness, regardless of what happens to them.

This is a condition that tends to surprise Lotto winners. They assume that $19 million will solve all of their problems, then before they know it they are back at their same old broke levels of happiness. Often worse. Lotto won't save us, because wherever we go, there we are; and whatever we have, we want something else.

Professor William B. Irvine explained this concept to me over Zoom.

> You're wired never to be satisfied because your ancestors who were satisfied didn't make it. The guy who said 'I'm going to sit out here on the savannah and appreciate what I have' — a lion ate that guy. The ones who were constantly incrementally looking to improve their situation did better. Our civilisation has outgrown the need for some of our wiring. The problem is, it's still there. We have to do our best to learn to live with it.

The desire to change, move, upgrade and ditch things sits deep within us. You wake up on Saturday morning with a desire. You need an asparagus steamer, and you need it now. It feels important. So you hustle out and buy it. It doesn't make you happy and you almost immediately need something else. Eventually, these desires fill our homes. Far from making life better, now we must work to find places to put them. Homeware stores should cut out the middle man and place skips at the exits so we can throw the crap out as we leave.

A quick look into the 100-year-old origins of planned obsolescence demonstrates how easily we are gamed when it comes to wanting things. In the 1920s, the American automotive market hit saturation point. Cars lasted a long time back then. Once you had one, you didn't need a new one for another fifteen years. Alfred P. Sloan Jr., an executive at General Motors, decided that the best way to get people to buy cars they didn't need was to release annual models with the year in their name. So, in 1922, the Chevrolet division slightly restyled the body covering of a nine-year-old vehicle and called it the 1923. They experienced a massive spike in sales.

Henry Ford, the founder of Ford Motor Company, whose Model T revolutionised transport after its introduction in 1908, hated the idea of model year changes. He wanted his company to focus on design integrity, engineering simplicity and quality production scaling. This honourable focus turned out to be a substantial commercial mistake. In 1923, Ford was by far the biggest seller of automobiles in the US, but General Motors quickly surpassed them — all because people desired the new thing with the latest number on it more than they valued quality engineering.

This new-number-new-year plan is still working on us. Next

time you 'need' a new phone, it might be worth questioning whether you desire it because of its new exciting features or its new incremental number. Is the latest super-expensive model that much better than the one a few numbers ago? When we base a purchase on something as tenuous as a changeable number, the joy we get from it is bound to be short-lived.

Regardless of our current desires or reasons for buying, once our basic needs have been met more purchasing isn't going to lead us to lasting happiness. We need more than *things* to achieve that. Yet most of us are caught in a cycle of want and disappointment. When it comes to the endless piles of objects we bring into our lives, we might ask ourselves: 'Why am I buying more crap when I already have a house, garage and storage unit full of crap?'

The Ancient Turkish slave and philosopher Epictetus (50–135 CE) said that

> freedom is not procured by a full enjoyment of what is desired, but by proving the desire to be a wrong one.
> —in *All the Works of Epictetus*, p. 329

Whole lifetimes can pass without acquiring the happiness that objects promise. This is because satisfaction doesn't come from getting more, but from learning to control our wants. One way to do this is to understand the craving. To focus on its true nature. Two and a half thousand years ago, a wealthy man called Siddhartha Gautama jumped off the hedonic treadmill, and changed the world.

* * *

Siddhartha was born into wealth around 600 BCE in what is now Nepal. He led a life of luxury up to the age of 29, when he started looking around outside the palace. On his journeys he saw a number of shocking sights. First he met a sick man, then an ageing man, and then a dying man. A realisation came to him: these poor people all represented inevitable parts of the human condition. His own wealth, power and possessions would not protect him from suffering. He too would get sick, would get old and would die.

Further on, he came across a holy man who was seeking a spiritual life among all this suffering. Impressed by the man's calmness, Siddhartha renounced his life of luxury and embarked on six years of intense spiritual practice and study. Despite all this, however, he remained deeply dissatisfied. His questions on life weren't being answered.

Despairing that he would never find inner peace, he slumped down under a fig tree in northern India. And there, it hit him that all things in the world — from ants to human beings — are unified by suffering. Any contentment he might find would come from within himself rather than from outside. We must change our outlook, not our circumstances. With this knowledge, Siddhartha Gautama attained enlightenment. He would become known as The Buddha, from the Pali and Sanskrit word for 'awakened'.

The Buddha's teachings can help us deal with our endless wanting in a number of ways. To start with, if we accept that suffering in life is unavoidable, we can lower our wants and expectations. Buddhist teacher Noah Rasheta puts it this way:

> Sex will disappoint us, youth will disappear, money and possessions won't spare us pain. The wise person should take care to grow completely at home with the ordinary shambles of existence. —in *No-nonsense Buddhism for Beginners*, p. 5

Gautama saw greed as one of the 'three poisons' that lead us to evil; the other two being hatred and ignorance. From a Buddhist perspective, greed is a problem because it motivates us to look outside of ourselves for happiness rather than within. Material possessions don't bring us the long-term joy we expect them to, and instead bring us suffering in their pursuit.

We mistakenly believe that our unhappiness comes from not having enough. We imagine that one day, if we could just get the right amount of things, we could finally relax and be happy. But no matter how much money, fame or power we get, we can't seem to find lasting contentment.

This is not to say that we should shun either possessions or success. Gautama believed that economic security was needed for inner peace; he believed strongly in hard work. But he also believed that everything should be balanced by internal choices, like cultivating compassion for others and seeking enlightenment. If we are too attached to *things*, we worry about them and suffer when we lose them. Gautama taught that there is nothing wrong with using material things to our advantage and the advantage of others, but we should not attach our happiness to them. Seeking more *things* for the purposes of happiness only leads to suffering, because a mental state filled with desire and greed will never find contentment. We should instead look for a state of inner mental tranquillity and spread that outwards: if you are well inside yourself, you will treat other people better and make the world a better place.

HOW TO FIGHT CRAVINGS

There is nothing wrong with desires in themselves; they motivate us. The problems come when we remain blind to their causes and outcomes. We can, instead, concentrate on our wants and become aware of every aspect of our desires. If you crave money, fame and possessions, it may be helpful to honestly ask yourself *why* you want them? If you desire a new car, and on closer inspection of that desire you discover that it's actually to impress others — you might want to reconsider the purchase.

Mehrab Reza is the founder of Adlantica, a US marketing

and creative agency that studies human desire in order to shift products. When he looked into why he'd bought a new Porsche Panamera, he realised that all the things he said made him want his dream car weren't actually true. It wasn't the engine, the top speed, or the handling — all that was just a story he was telling himself. When he really focused on the desire honestly, he realised:

> To be brutally honest, the human desire I was seeking to satisfy was the desire to attain more social status, signal success to others, to impress my friends . . . I'm not proud of myself for that. —in 'The basic human desires that drive all purchasing decisions'

To survive in a modern society, we have to purchase things or we will starve. When a big desire appears — outside of what we need to survive — we will create a story for ourselves, and others, that justifies going through with the purchase. That story is rarely the real reason for the purchase. If we zone right in on the desire and be really honest with ourselves, we may find that we don't like our true motives.

As Noah Rasheta teaches:

> Simply following our desires without taking time to understand them leads to destructive behavior and mental confusion. —in *No-nonsense Buddhism for Beginners*, p. 37

If we are honest with ourselves and mindful of the real reasons for our desires, we might not like what we see and may look for another path to happiness.

* * *

Epictetus believed that much of our want for worldly things comes from a skewed perspective. We look fondly at things we don't have when we should do the same for the things we do. It's easier to gain happiness if we learn to want what we already have. Say you find yourself fantasising about an expensive kitchen renovation; you flick through pictures of the most beautiful tiles, taps and plumbed refrigerators available. A better plan is to look in the other direction. Imagine yourself as one of the hundreds of millions around the world who don't have hot and cold running water at all. Flick through pictures of people in impoverished nations. Imagine yourself walking to a river kilometres away and carrying the day's water back home on your head. With a different comparison, we can learn to feel grateful for what we have and less desirous of the things we don't need.

At spare moments during the day, you could make it a point to contemplate the loss of whatever you value in life. Imagine those things stolen or broken. Engaging in such contemplation changes your outlook. It can make you realise — if only for a time — how lucky you are. You might experience gratitude instead of want.

We spend a lot of our lives thinking about houses. Some of us scroll endlessly through property listings looking for something bigger with a better view. I lived for a year in a leaky 2x1.5-metre shed on Ariki Street in Auckland. The door didn't close, the power was intermittent, there were rats living below the floorboards, many of which were missing, and my girlfriend broke up with me after spending one night there. My current house feels a lot better when I compare it to that shed rather than to other people's mansions.

And even that shed is better than what some people have. When I was in India recently, I saw two homeless children with no shoes rummaging through a street-side rubbish pile. If I bring those poor souls to mind, how can I be unhappy with where I live and what I own? It may not be a palace, but it's not literally a dump. Those children in the rubbish pile would be amazed if they found out that we not only feel dissatisfied with all we have in life, which is more than they could hope for, but that we want much more.

Former American basketball player Shaquille O'Neal's dad understands downward comparison. On his Big Podcast, Shaquille shared this story. One day after a game he goes home to New York and complains about his situation in the NBA. His father doesn't like this, and the next day takes him in a car to see a homeless family. He calls Shaq a spoilt brat for complaining and points out that he has a mansion and flies in a private jet, while these people don't even know where their next meal is coming from.

Shaq was unhappy because he was looking in the wrong direction. His dad told him to get out of the car, make a few phone calls and get the family an apartment. And he did. Shaq stopped complaining about his position in life (well not to his dad anyway).

* * *

I am not saying that purchasing will never bring you joy, but if happiness is the goal of your spending it is worth being mindful of why and where you are throwing your money. A 2020 paper called 'Spending on doing promotes more moment-to-moment happiness than spending on having' outlined research conducted by a team led by Amit Kumar. They split 2635 adults into two groups. One group was the 'material group' and the other the 'experiential group'. The material group bought items such as furniture, jewellery and clothing. The other group went to restaurants, sports games and participated in various experiences. Throughout the study, the researchers randomly texted participants to ask them how they felt. And they found that happiness was higher for the participants who consumed experiential purchases than for those who consumed material ones, regardless of the cost of the item.

The participants were happier with experiential purchases before, during and after. The value of material things seemed to diminish over time, while the value of experiences seemed to grow in the remembering. Kumar summed up the study this way:

> If you want to be happier, it might be wise to shift some of your consumption away from material goods and a bit more toward experiences. That would likely lead to greater well-being. —quoted on UT News website, 9 March 2020

Of course, experiences don't solve every problem. You can spend a lot and get nothing if you are not in the right state of mind. In a surprisingly deep 2019 *Saturday Night Live* skit, Adam Sandler, playing Italian tour operator Joe Romano, tells viewers how on his tours he can take you to the most beautiful places on Earth — fishing in Sorrento, hiking the cliffs of the Amalfi Coast. But you are still going to be you on the holiday. If you are unhappy where you are and you get on a plane, the same sad you will land at your destination. A holiday is just you in a new place — it doesn't make you a new person. He explains that holidays can do a lot, like help you unwind, but they won't solve how you behave with others, or your baseline mood.

One simple way we can experience more enjoyment on holiday is by choosing what we focus on. When walking around a new area, some of us stare at the beachfront houses we wish we owned. *If only I could win Lotto*, you think, *I could buy that place and enjoy that view.* Or: *If only I had purchased here 25 years ago when it was worth next to nothing. That view could have been mine.* You can spend your time wishing you owned the house, or you can turn around and enjoy the view now, while you have it. You can long for that sweet access to the water they have, or just go for a swim. Being at the beach in the first place is a great position to be in, so you might as well enjoy it how you have it. Things could always be more opulent, but they could also be so much worse. A great way to ruin a holiday is to spend it wishing everything was better.

HAVING ENOUGH

The other day, we were driving in our latest vehicle and my sons started talking about how much they missed the car three cars ago. The one we just *had* to get rid of to make life better. They were right; that was a perfectly good car.

Toyota, Ford, BMW, Mercedes, Ferrari, Aston Martin, Bentley, Maserati, Suzuki Swift, a new watch, a bespangled dog collar, an $89 dishwashing liquid dispenser: these things are all beautiful, but — unfortunately — none of them will solve your emotional problems.

Chapter Nine

Annoyed?

An irritating human in his mid-thirties is standing beside me on the sideline of a kids' football match. He's wealthy and won't shut up about it. This man, who I have dubbed Punisher McSkimmons, is showing off about his new tennis court and swimming pool. Apparently, he spent more than the 'price of the average home' on a complex drainage system. He goes on to inform everyone nearby that it was all worth it. His son is now 'incredible' at tennis.

After going on for an additional 30 minutes about an upcoming European holiday, McSkimmons offers to get coffees for all the parents watching. This is preceded by a lengthy explanation of his amazing home coffee set-up: 'It's better than you'll get at any cafe in the country.' Apparently he imported his espresso machine from Italy. It is 'not the kind of crap you can buy in a mall'. I ask for a flat white; McSkimmons describes this as a 'crime of a drink' and leaves.

I turn to the mum beside me and quip, sarcastically, 'So

Punisher McSkimmons's new tennis court is the best tennis court in the history of tennis courts — who would have thought? What a punisher.' The woman doesn't laugh at either my observation or the clever nickname I have made up; she just looks straight ahead and, with mild disgust, mutters, 'Do you have to go on about this every week?'

This is an unexpected turn of events. I thought *everyone* found McSkimmons annoying. In an attempt to defend myself, I whinge, 'But Punisher McSkimmons goes on and on about his stuff every week.'

She answers, 'Why do you care so much? It's not killing you.' She has me on the ropes. I have no idea why I care so much. So I make something up. I tell her I just want to watch our kids play, not hear how rich he is.

'Well, watch them. Jesus, Matt. No one knows what you are talking about with your nicknames. You're making these games awkward for the rest of us. If you have a problem, just say it to his face.'

To her *I* am the annoying parent at these games, not Punisher McSkimmons. She probably has a nickname for me, too, like 'Matthew Whingedick'. Others probably discuss how annoying I am. This is a terrible turn of events.

Being annoyed is one thing; being so annoyed that *you* become annoying is another.

* * *

Annoyance is a cousin to anger. And like its cuz, it's a natural and adaptive response to the world around us. If something messes with our expectations, concentration, or sense of control, we feel annoyed. Annoyance can be triggered by social interactions, noises, impediments, our environment, or stuff we make up in our heads. In their book *Annoying: The science of what bugs us*, Joe Palca and Flora Lichtman found three essential qualities that they believe must be present for annoyance.

First: it must be noxious without being physically harmful. A housefly buzzing around your head is unpleasant, but it won't kill you — so it's annoying. Second: it must be unpredictable and intermittent. The loud ticking of a clock may be annoying at first, or if it's stopping and starting, but with constant exposure over time it ceases to be noticeable.

We have lots of loud cicadas in New Zealand. The males have pairs of small ribbed membranes that they flex rapidly, producing multiple clicks. In the summer, with thousands of them going at once, it gets noisy. We would probably get annoyed if it came in short bursts. But the little buggers just go on and on, so we don't really notice them. Some overseas film and TV productions receiving New Zealand footage assume that a technical problem has created loud static in the audio. I once got an annoyed call from a UK-based producer accusing us of cocking up our sound recording. I told her that the constant buzzing she was hearing on the tape 'is just the sound of the great New Zealand summer'. This didn't help. Whether or not we Kiwis notice our unruly cicadas, the audio was unusable.

The third and final essential quality of annoyance is unpredictability. To be truly annoying, something has to persist for an uncertain period of time. We can deal with a food delivery being 20 minutes late if we are informed of the delay. It becomes annoying if we're left in the dark as to when our meal will actually arrive.

Annoyance does, of course, have utility. Psychologist and author of *Complaining, Teasing, and Other Annoying Behaviors* Robin Kowalski explains that the feeling of annoyance is signalling that things need to be done, that something is getting in the way of our goals or preferences. It's an emotion that exists to push us towards action.

At its most useful, annoyance motivates us to make things better. If a door is banging in the wind, annoyance might prompt you to close it and prevent a whole lot of rain coming in. If you're losing concentration in the office because someone is talking a lot, annoyance might motivate you to ask them nicely to keep it down. Annoyance at the sound of a buzzing mosquito might motivate you to squash it before it gives you malaria.

Some people encounter irksome noises, smells and people everywhere they go; others glide through life undistracted. Those who are easily annoyed are sometimes described as petty. This was me for many years. I couldn't stand being around one co-worker because she held her hands too high in conversations. She was like Will Ferrell in the movie *Talladega Nights: The Ballad of Ricky Bobby* — during his first TV interview, his hands kept involuntarily rising into shot. I couldn't be in a room with another colleague at a different workplace because he said sorry too much. I was particularly annoyed when he said sorry for saying sorry. If, like me, you find yourself dealing with an inordinate number of aggravating people, you might want to consider the following adage: *If you run into an arsehole in the morning, they might be an arsehole. If you run into arseholes all day — you are probably the arsehole.*

Annoyance may not seem like a major problem at first, but if it continues it can suck the joy out of life. Anger might bring things to a head; annoyance can sit unresolved, simmering away for years, making your work, social and home life consistently less enjoyable. It's an emotion that feels uncomfortable by its nature, leads to poor decisions and takes up mental space that could be used on more productive endeavours, relaxation or socialisation. It also snowballs. If we allow ourselves to be annoyed at a thing, we will find more reasons to be annoyed. If we start to do nasty things to the people who annoy us, soon we are disliking them more and doing more nasty things. It can cause us to miss out on potential friendships, turn us into the bad guys and flip positive experiences into negative ones.

In the past few years I've found ways to change my behaviour and perspective in an attempt to remove unhelpful annoyance from my life. As it turns out, you can usually choose to perceive events such that they don't annoy you. Learning a little tolerance can open up your world.

AVOIDING ANNOYANCE

> Tell yourself: the people I deal with today will be meddling, ungrateful, arrogant, dishonest, jealous and surly. —Marcus Aurelius, *Meditations*, p. 17

Annoyance is often the result of unrealised expectations. You work hard and expect thanks — and instead receive complaints. You expect support, and get abandoned. You trust someone, and they lie. Marcus suggests that instead of expecting things to align with our wishes, we should resign ourselves to the failings of others.

The fact that you'll encounter irritating people shouldn't come as a surprise. They're everywhere. But if you anticipate potential bad behaviour, you increase your ability to deal with it constructively.

You may already know what behaviours set you off. Ungrateful drivers used to get me going. There's one street I travel down multiple times a week. It's two-way but narrow, so if there's a car coming from the other direction one of us has to pull over. If a driver performs this courtesy, I wave thanks as I go by; it's the least I can do for someone who's stopped moving so that I can continue. However, when *I* stop and the other driver doesn't wave, I used to get annoyed. I'd sit there thinking, in advance, 'You better wave, you bastard.' If they didn't, I'd swing my head around and flash them the stink-eye. Now, before I turn down this street, I accept in my heart that some people aren't going to wave. Who knows why? Maybe they are bad people, maybe they are missing an arm. Their reasons are irrelevant. I will continue to wave because it's the right thing to do.

Each morning, you might take a moment to accept that there will be aggravating people in your life today. Remind yourself that becoming annoyed is weak and counterproductive. Resolve to deal with whatever happens in a virtuous manner. Do this every day, and you might make your little world a better place. Maybe someone at your workplace spends 80% of their working day vaping on the street. Forgive their wrongdoing in advance so that you can spend your energy elsewhere.

If we are reminding ourselves in the morning what to expect throughout the day, we could also do what Seneca suggests and evaluate how we did at the end of the day. He would review everything with an eye for improvement.

You may well look back and find things you could have done better. You might also find reasons to praise yourself. If someone was unreasonable and you worked through the situation in a logical, advantageous way for all — then great. But if you got annoyed, made up a stupid nickname for a person and attempted to backstab them to an innocent mum on a sports sideline, you might mark yourself down a few points. When we regularly reflect on our actions, we may see patterns; and in that case we can make plans to react in a more tolerant fashion in the future. Do this and we can go to sleep feeling proud.

Like everyone else on Earth, Seneca was far from perfect; he often found fault in himself. On one famous occasion outlined by Professor Irvine in *A Guide to the Good Life*, Seneca became annoyed when he wasn't seated in a more honoured place at a banquet. Reflecting on it that night, he realised that rather than enjoying himself and the delicious food on offer, he had spent the banquet feeling irritated at those who had planned the seating and at those in better seats than him. This is how he assessed his behaviour:

> You lunatic, what difference does it make what part of the couch you put your weight on? (p. 120)

* * *

It's not just people that annoy us. We can find tables, doors, lights, and hard-to-open chip packets irritating. In a 1948 column for the English magazine *The Spectator*, humourist Paul Jennings gave this behaviour the name 'resistentialism'. He described our interactions with inanimate objects as an ongoing war. According to Jennings, the little annoyances caused by objects are the battles of this wider conflict. This is, of course, silly. They may be poorly designed, or in the wrong place — but outside of horror movies, inanimate objects don't run agendas against us. If we find ourselves annoyed at lost keys, squeaky chairs and ripped pants, we are personifying them.

In his book *The Consolations of Philosophy*, Alain de Botton claims that we get annoyed 'because of an implicit belief in a world in which remote controls do not get mislaid' (p. 84). In reality things don't naturally fall in line with the needs of modern humans. Take the yearly untangling of Christmas lights. It's annoying because somewhere deep down we believe we live in a universe where lights stay in a perfect formation. When in fact we live in one that moves towards chaos. Entropy is a measure of the degree of randomness or disorganisation within a system, and it tends to increase over time.

Chris Smith from The Naked Scientists website described the Christmas lights situation in a 2017 interview with Hugh Hunt, Professor of Engineering, Dynamics and Vibration at the University of Cambridge:

> There's one organised way to have your lights, but there are many many ways to have your lights in a disorganised way. So the odds are, that they're not going to stay organised for very long unless you take enormous steps to make sure.

The universe doesn't care if your lights end up in a horrible, screwed-up unsolvable mess; it's all the same to the cosmos. The only entity with an emotional investment in the state of those lights is the one untangling them. If you want your lights to remain in an orderly fashion, input anti-chaos energy into the system by rolling them up carefully at the end of the festive season.

If we accept that we live in a world where remote controls go missing and Christmas lights get tangled, there is no reason to feel personally set upon when they do. Lost keys don't reappear because you are annoyed at them. A broken dishwasher doesn't start working again because you called it 'a piece of shit', and Alexa doesn't feel bad because it played 'Santa Baby' when you asked for 'Smells Like Teen Spirit'. Instead of becoming annoyed after the fact, you could calmly put steps in place for the future. Make a spot where you return the remote and keys. Rinse dishes before you put them in the dishwasher so they don't block the drainage. Research the quality of devices before you buy them.

When artificial intelligence finally becomes sentient, we may have to re-evaluate things. If we one day have a toaster with the empirical intelligence to contemplate, experience and perceive the world around it just as humans do, then it would make more sense to call it names when it burns our toast. Until then, irritation directed at inanimate objects is a waste of time and energy.

This isn't to say that annoyance at other humans is a good use of our time. Marcus Aurelius believed that you should choose not to be affected by *anything* or *anyone*.

> You don't have to turn this into something. It doesn't have to upset you. Things can't shape our decisions by themselves. —in *Meditations*, p. 81

Does the noise from across the road, the way a friend sits on the couch, a delay in the arrival of a package, or any other non-life-threatening occurrence have to become a *thing*? Is it worth any of your time and energy? According to Marcus, we always have the option not to engage. To use a cricketing metaphor, you can choose to 'let it go through to the keeper'. It's a simple but effective option. You can tell yourself, inside your head — preferably using your first name like a friend would — 'Matt, don't worry about it. Move on.'

If this isn't working, there are other ways we can reframe our thinking and move away from irritation.

Look back on now: Mentalist Derren Brown, author of *A Book of Secrets*, suggests jumping forward in your imagination and taking a retrospective look at the people you are annoyed with. Try seeing them now as if you were remembering them at the end of your life, or at the end of their lives. By doing this, you might feel a nostalgic warmth towards them. Annoyance generally disappears when attending a person's funeral. In hindsight, Brown sees the annoying people in his life with a new fondness.

We have a short time on this planet, and we spend most of it with a relatively small group of humans. Your family, your school, your workplace, your neighbourhood: these are your people. They're not perfect, and you aren't either. There are likely better specimens out there, but these are the characters who populate your particular life. These individuals, even ones who annoy you, are yours. They are the people you will spend a portion of your life with. This is your tribe, your annoying people. Viewing things this way can take the edge off them.

To take Brown's method a step further, you could picture the irksome people not only as the characters who populate your life, but also as the cast of your sitcom. Their foibles, however challenging, are essential for your day-to-day story. Is the person you sit beside at work unbearable, or are they your equivalent of Kramer from *Seinfeld*, Tracy Jordan from *30 Rock* or Dwight Schrute from *The Office*? Are they to be avoided, or do they generate the situations that make life interesting? If you see annoying people as characters, you may start to look forward to their quirks rather than run away from them. It would be nice if the people I annoy could see their way to viewing me as a delightful cross between Barney Gumble (the fat burping drunk from *The Simpsons*), Abed Nadir (the awkward but lovable nerd from *Community*) and George Costanza (the stocky neurotic loser from *Seinfeld*).

Find your anti-mentor: Sitcoms can help us fight annoyance in other ways. Larry David's *Curb Your Enthusiasm* is one of the funniest shows ever made; it's also an in-depth investigation of annoyance. Across more than two decades on the air, Larry has been annoyed at being asked to take off his shoes, outdated magazines in waiting rooms, people who force caterers to wear bow-ties, wobbly tables, airplane seat 'encroachment', trick-ortreaters who don't wear costumes, people who say 'Happy New Year' after January 4th, people who hog all the cabinet space in a shared kitchen, not enough cashews in a snack mix, appetiser skewers, people who travel in shorts, and people who take too many free samples. I have to pause the show at least once an episode to relieve the tension. I've screamed 'Just let it go, Larry!' at the TV multiple times. *Curb* is a cautionary tale on how things spiral out of control if you let them annoy you.

Feeling annoyed? Try saying to yourself: 'You're being Larry David! Just let it go! This is not going to turn out well.' If Larry doesn't do it for you, there are easily irritated, grumpy people in everyone's real lives who will make excellent anti-mentors.

Assume the best: We can become annoyed at people out of ignorance, pettiness or misunderstanding. One afternoon, the mother of my children texts me: 'Are you picking the kids up from school?' Being the open wound I was at the time, I interpret this to mean a snarky 'Are you going to pick the kids up from school or are you out drinking with your mates, you slack, irresponsible loser?' So I reply: 'Yes. I am picking up the kids as I said I would. I am a good dad in case you haven't noticed. I do more than my bit.'

After sending that, I realised that a second text had come through. It read: 'Because I can't remember if I said I would get them. Sorry. Also, do you want to come round? I am having a BBQ. It should be fun. I bought you steak.' I had created my own annoyance out of thin air — an emotional own-goal due to a petty assumption. If, instead, I had chosen a neutral or positive interpretation of the communication, there would have been no annoyance to be had.

We can't read other people's minds, so assuming that we have been impeded, judged or told off is a risky way to live. If your default assumption is that people mean well, you will be less annoyed. If they did mean to say something annoying, it's not the end of the world if we fail to attribute that to them.

Be objective: The irritation you feel is unlikely to be based on an unshakeable moral truth. Your feelings are largely subjective in nature. If a Kiwi family visits a beach where only one other family is present, we'll tend to throw down our towels a discreet distance away. In some Mediterranean countries, though, plopping down right next door is the norm. Your annoyance at a family who gets too close may be a product of your upbringing. It might be worth asking: Why do I really care about this? Why is it annoying? Is there any damage being done here, or is it just the breaking of an arbitrarily assigned norm? You've always been around people who set up a long way away and these people have set up close, so you feel annoyed. This could easily be reframed as we always set up a long way away, they have set up close — what does it matter?

A few years ago I went camping with my fantastic older sister at Purakaunui Bay in New Zealand's lower South Island. When we arrived at the isolated beach, she spotted some campers barely visible in the distance. With great annoyance, she complained, 'Well I guess we *don't* have the beach to ourselves.' I had recently been to Waikiki Beach in Honolulu, every inch of which was covered with seething humanity. With that experience fresh in my mind, I found it hard to rustle up any annoyance at a couple of campers two kilometres away.

Don't ask for it: It might be your own behaviour that is causing your annoyance. If you move to a house beside a stadium that's been there for over a hundred years, like Eden Park in Auckland, it would be silly to get annoyed at the noise. In the same way, if you find yourself irritated at someone on social media, it might help to remember that you don't have to be there. Delete the apps.

Remember that you're also annoying: If someone is annoying you, try asking yourself whether you have done that very thing yourself. If you're at a dinner party and your friend's partner is too loud, you could ask yourself whether you have ever got rowdy before. If someone constantly makes unfunny, annoying jokes, ask yourself: 'Am I always an absolute crack-up?' If someone talks about themselves too much, ask yourself how often you share personal stories. Chances are, you're committing the same offences that annoy you. If you admit that you are guilty of the same thing, then it is harder to remain annoyed.

Marcus put it another way in *Meditations*:

> It's silly to try to escape other people's faults. They are inescapable. Just try to escape your own. (p. 97)

Is it worth it? Is an indiscretion worth the time and energy you are committing to it? Is the fact that you can hear the neighbours talking loudly over the fence really, in the scheme of things, *that* bad? Do you really need to start a war with them over it? Is the way a person eats their food worth you leaving the table and missing out on good conversation?

Are you hungover? Your irritation might be a physical problem manifesting in a mental condition. If you feel your annoyance rising, before acting, try asking yourself: Am I hungover? Or stressed, tired, unhealthy, or overweight? Do I need to do a number 2? Is it blue Monday or ecky Tuesday? If you've been out late, maybe factor that in and adjust your levels of human tolerance accordingly.

Annoyance is often more about our own mental and emotional physical condition than the other person's behaviour. On a good day, a car alarm going off down the street might be simply a matter of interest; on a bad day, we can find it unbearably annoying. When we are not running at 100%, an innocent-until-proven-guilty approach is probably best. Sentencing an innocent person to our snarkiness just because we're having a bad day makes *us* the bad guys.

Just say something: Much of our annoyance stems from cowardice. If you spend your days annoyed at the way someone is behaving but never bring that matter up with them, that's on you. Most people don't want to be annoying. If a topic is raised in the right way, they might happily change their behaviour. If we find ourselves bitching and backstabbing but never raising the issue, then we deserve to remain annoyed.

THE CASE FOR PUNISHER MCSKIMMONS

That lovely mum who didn't like me on the sideline of my kid's football game was right: who cares if Punisher McSkimmons talks about his new tennis court? When he returns with my flat white, I simply choose not to be annoyed by him. Instead of rolling my eyes as he discusses his successful life, I engage.

To my amazement, we have a decent conversation. Over time, I grow to enjoy Punisher McSkimmons's sideline company. It turns out he's a weird, generous and intelligent guy with all kinds of interesting tastes. As I get to know him, I realise he was not showing off about his pool and tennis court — he was talking from his perspective as a successful engineer. The problem was mine. My lack of tolerance, along with jealousy and a hangover.

Remaining annoyed with Punisher McSkimmons could have ruined my enjoyment of my son's sport. It could have prevented me from making a new friend. The solution was so simple. All I had to do was find a way not to be annoyed.

Chapter Ten

Bored?

One of my sons loves swimming in the ocean. Spending time with him in the water is about the most life-affirming thing I can imagine. It's a gift. I feel so lucky to be with him, battling the waves. Like most parents with kids, I am conscious that he's growing up fast and won't be around as much in a few years. I know I will miss him a lot when he heads off to forge his own path in life; the universe doesn't create better people than my boys.

To be in beautiful nature with someone I love is special. The sea, the blue sky. As we pound through the surf, we laugh and smile at each other whenever our heads appear above the water at the same time. A perfect day.

Then, from out of nowhere, the thought appears in my head: 'Get out, you're bored.' Suddenly all I want to do is go somewhere else. My boy would stay in for hours, but I have a deep desire to bail after ten minutes. Why? There is nowhere I have to be. Why would I get bored, doing the good stuff?

Before you know it we are in the car, racing away from that wholesome marine experience towards somewhere else, knowing that we will arrive and I will want to leave there, too. Wherever I am, I feel the need to go. Unless, of course, that place is on the couch watching YouTube clips — then I'm good for hours. If I'm drinking, I might be good for days. When I'm staring into my phone, there are no deep impulses demanding that I put it down.

Feelings of restlessness are particularly disappointing when we're at the places we want to be. Say you're at a concert; you've been looking forward to it, you're loving it, then suddenly you start hoping it will end. You have flown there, booked a hotel, spent a fortune, and all you can think is: 'How many songs are left so I can go?'

Looking back on time spent swimming with your child is the kind of thing that brings satisfaction in life. We are unlikely to look back fondly on the hours we spend scrolling 60-second videos. Yet the unhealthy activities pull us in, and the beautiful, meaningful ones push us away. How many holidays, books, lessons, deep conversations, walks and adventures with the people we love do we miss out on because we lack the patience and attention to stick around and enjoy them? Why are so many of us so bored?

* * *

In his book *Boredom: A lively history*, Peter Toohey outlines the two types of boredom that most people recognise. The first is how you might feel during a long speech, a school assembly, or while waiting in line. The kind that makes us want to leave wherever we are. The second is existential boredom, which can infect your very existence.

I addressed the existential type as best as I could in the earlier chapter on dissatisfaction; the boredom we are talking about here is the first variety; the type that had me throwing rocks at trees when I was alone on the farm growing up. The kind that can, unfortunately, encourage you to walk away from the most worthwhile parts of your life.

However, like most of the unpleasant feelings we have, boredom has utility in our lives. Some experts think that far from avoiding it, we should actively seek it out.

THE CASE FOR BOREDOM

In his book *The Power of Boredom*, Mark A. Hawkins argues that boredom can be used to motivate us to enhance our lives. He claims boredom (much like annoyance) is a signal that something needs to be done. Instead of seeing it as a negative emotion to be avoided, he suggests using it as a catalyst for creativity and innovation. Instead of hiding from it, with booze, drugs, food or digital devices, we should allow it into our lives. Then, with nothing else going on, creativity, hobbies or whole careers might fill the gap.

Instead of jumping on your phone (or any other external stimulation), you might let yourself get so bored that you feel compelled to write, form a band, start a business, come up with a joke, or ask someone out on a date. It's possible to embrace the stillness and allow boredom to become a force that pushes us towards more meaningful things.

In 2016, Neil Gaiman, author of the novels *Good Omens*, *Stardust* and *American Gods*, was asked by Seth Meyers on his late-night show for some advice for young writers. He replied that if you are looking for a good idea for a book, you might want to try getting so bored that your brain starts telling you an interesting story. Jimi Hendrix famously came up with his innovative guitar style because he was 'bored shitless' playing conservatively in a suit and tie behind artists like The Isley Brothers and Curtis Knight. Isaac Newton invented calculus in the summer of 1663 because he was bored hiding at home from a plague outbreak in London. On a much less significant note, I'm pretty sure it was painful small-town boredom that pushed me and my teenage friends to start shooting the violent short films that started me on the career I am still in today.

* * *

There is, however, an obvious problem with this thinking. If you are spurred to inspiration by boredom, that's great — but what if your boredom levels have become calibrated so that you can't get anything productive done? Your book idea or your brand-new branch of mathematics will probably involve some hard, dull work to bring into existence. There are repetitive things we need to stick with to reach our long-term goals.

Business writer Shane Parrish discusses this in a 2022 article entitled 'Boredom & Impatience'. He points out that the way we get good at things is to practise the basics for a very long time. You struggle to do that if you are always craving excitement in the present. Boredom can push you away from doing what you need to do now to become great later.

This kind of dedication has become harder to find in recent decades. We are becoming more and more distracted. In a 2023 interview with the podcast Speaking of Psychology, Gloria Mark, a professor of informatics at the University of California, Irvine, discusses our falling attention span. In 2004, researchers tracked how quickly we turn away from a single activity. The average attention span back then was two and a half minutes. By 2012 it was down to 75 seconds. At the time of writing, the average is just 47 seconds.

These plummeting figures are being blamed on lives tethered to smartphones and computers. We have powerful distraction machines with us *all the time*. They are too entertaining, and as a result we are cutting and running more and more quickly from other things in our lives. A lack of boredom is becoming a problem; we'll do anything to avoid downtime. You hardly ever see people sitting at a bus stop or in the back of an Uber just looking around — everyone is staring down at their phones. I've held off going to the bathroom, to the point of risking an 'accident', as I ran around in a mad panic looking for my phone. God forbid sitting on a seat in silence for a few minutes! Yet it was committing to doing that very thing for ten minutes every day that ultimately solved my perpetual restlessness.

On the surface there would appear to be few things in this world more boring than meditation. When you start a mindfulness practice it's just you, with your eyes closed, concentrating on your breath. But more and more people are doing it. According to Laura Smith on The Good Body website, the number of meditators in the US has tripled since 2013, and the US meditation and mindfulness industry is estimated to be worth $2.7 billion.

In his book *Waking Up*, neuroscientist Sam Harris claims mindfulness practice improves blood pressure, cortisol (stress hormone) levels and immune function. It also lowers anxiety, emotional reactivity and neuroticism and increases subjective wellbeing. However, I believe that the best outcome of a mindfulness practice is that it gives you the tools to make the boring things in your life not just bearable, but fun.

Meditation can increase your attention span outside of practice to a point where you don't get bored when nothing is happening. Once you learn how to distance yourself from the constant flood of thoughts that bubble up from within your brain and take you away, life becomes a lot easier. You can sit back from the thoughts that tell you to be somewhere else, do something else, or worry about something else. You can just *be* for periods of time. You can keep at things you would normally walk away from.

When we build up our mindfulness muscles, we can step back mentally, wake up and experience the world as it is whenever we need to. We can appreciate the opening of a door, the wonder of driving a car, or the taste of simple foods.

All the guidance you need to start a mindfulness practice is readily available in apps, books and on YouTube channels. But the basics are simple. Normally you begin by paying attention to your breath as it goes in and out. When your mind wanders from this task, simply return to focusing on your breath without judgement. Paying attention to the breath anchors you in the present moment. It's tough at the start, but you soon grow the skills of mindfulness. Your powers of attention increase. Eventually you reach moments of bliss in which you can experience the input of your senses from a place behind your ego. When thoughts arise, you can observe them from a distance as they disappear. It's cool.

In my experience, a daily practice of 10 to 20 minutes brings real-life advantages. If you can't sleep and find yourself lying in bed bored, mindfulness can help you accept the situation, concentrate on your breathing and enjoy just existing until you drift off. Things like waiting in line become less of a problem; you just lean in to mindfulness and become aware of the sensations and sounds all around you. There is plenty going on, even when it appears that nothing is.

With an increased ability to pay attention, you can stick with boring work that needs to be done; you can continue to exercise when your brain starts telling you to leave; you can zone in on the beauty of spending time with your family. You can happily go to the bathroom without your phone. Meditation is worth doing because it makes life less boring.

This does, however, raise a paradox. Meditation is discovering that life exists in the immediate moment. So if you meditate with a goal — like self-improvement — in mind, then you're looking to the future and, as such, you're not meditating. English philosophical entertainer and mind-blower Alan Watts believed that the only way round this paradox was to meditate simply because it's fun. Arriving in the moment is a buzz. All the positive results that come as a result of the meditation — like feeling calmer, less bored and more satisfied — occur in the future. So they aren't part of the practice of spending time in the present.

This may be true, but that's not how I do it. I do, in fact, meditate to make my life better. I might be doing it wrong — it might not be 'pure' meditation — but it seems to be working. I used to be incapable of sitting on a couch for five minutes without entertainment; now I can enjoy an hour of weight training, yoga class, or a run in silence without watching the clock. At this very moment I am writing a book and haven't been distracted for ages. I may be a long way from full enlightenment, but I am a hell of a lot less bored with the good and real things in life.

A GOOD TIME

I was walking with my son last week (not the one from the ocean; the other one). We were talking about movies, music and life. It was wholesome father-and-son time, the kind of thing I want to be spending my life doing. As usual, I felt a powerful urge to do something else.

I took a second to become mindful of my thoughts. I observed that 'leave now' emotion and watched it until it disappeared. I rode it out. The urge to go went, and I was no longer bored.

My son and I walked on, chatting. Five minutes later, the urge to gap came back; I rode that one out, too. This time I got 30 minutes before my brain demanded an exit. A five-minute walk turned into 45 minutes of quality time with one of the people I love most in the world.

It was beautiful. Chances are he was bored out of his mind — but I wasn't.

Chapter Eleven

Worried?

It's the 1980s and we kids are really into Walkmans, basketball boots and worrying whether we'll die in a horrible, fiery nuclear apocalypse. The USA and the USSR hate each other and will likely blow up the world any day now. As far as I know there are no intercontinental ballistic missiles pointed at my small town at the bottom of New Zealand's South Island, but this is nothing to celebrate. We're told the post-attack nuclear winter will get us anyway. It might even be worse for those of us outside the initial firestorm. We will likely experience a slower, nastier death. Experts worry about severe and prolonged global climatic cooling, irradiated food, toxic ash falling from the sky, mutated offspring and a return to a cruel, medieval way of life. We are told that rusty ships packed with heavily armed northern-hemisphere survivors will arrive on our shores riddled with radiation and intent on enslaving and poisoning us.

Mrs Tipene, my teacher at Maori Hill Primary School in Dunedin, has two copies of the Raymond Briggs graphic novel

When the Wind Blows. Sitting at our little desks, my class listens in stunned horror as she shares this grim tale of a suburban British couple's attempt to survive nuclear fallout. The second copy is handed around so we can enjoy the deeply depressing illustrations up close. She tells us that this is our future if we don't do something to stop it. A tough task for a group of little kids at the bottom of the world. It seems unlikely that we hold the kind of geopolitical power needed to turn things around.

The movies of the day offer little hope. Matthew Broderick only just avoids World War III in *War Games*; the Australian/British made-for-TV *Threads* shows the grim effects of nuclear war on Sheffield; and then there's a slightly lighter ABC version, *The Day After*, in which everyone dies. There's also the Mel Gibson post-apocalyptic actioner *Mad Max Beyond Thunderdome*, showcasing a nuked Australia, with its catchy chart-topping Tina Turner theme song 'We Don't Need Another Hero'. Even closer to home, the post-nuke movie *Battletruck* uses our very own province of Otago for its horror waste-land.

In his 1986 paper 'Children's and adolescents' perceptions of the threat of nuclear war', William R. Beardslee reviewed studies in this area. In 1978, children were asked the broad question: 'What does the word "nuclear" bring to mind?' Here are some of the responses: big grey clouds, pipes and smokestacks, red warning lights, dead wildlife, dead humans, violence, danger, sadness, explosions, cancer, waste, bombs, pollution, darkness, the world's final demise.

These answers sum up the way we are feeling in New Zealand. While at the supermarket one day, my mother asks me why I look so worried. I answer: 'Nuclear war.'

* * *

We use the terms 'worry' and 'anxiety' interchangeably. While they both involve concern and unease, the way we experience them and their impact differ significantly.

According to Arash Emamzadeh on the website Psychology Today, worry is specific, while anxiety is more general. So you might worry about being on time for your flight, but feel anxious about travel as a whole. Worry is focused on thoughts in our heads; anxiety is a visceral experience that we feel throughout our entire bodies.

Worry also gets confused with preparation. While worrying might feel like you're preparing for the future, you might not be. Preparation is the human superpower that created civilisation; worrying is mostly just a spinning of mental wheels. We have succeeded as a species because of our ability to resist the immediate reward in favour of working, designing, saving and building. You can sit inside worrying about the state of your house, or you can make a plan to paint it, which is what I am currently doing. It's a big job — especially the preparation — but now that I am doing it, I am much less worried about future leaks. You can spend time worrying that someone younger or seemingly better than you might take your job, or you can resolve to do your best, be a pleasure to work with, and let the chips fall as they may. It's better than the standard approach of constant worrying mixed with seething resentment and bitching about your competition. That method tends to hasten your demise, strip you of your dignity and turn you into such a grumpy, unproductive bastard that everyone is pleased to see you go.

Worry may motivate you to make a plan, but worry isn't the work in itself. Some of us carry the false belief that if we ruminate on every coming possibility, we can control outcomes. But dwelling on endless unfortunate possibilities is simply procrastination. Planning is a constructive process that allows us to lay out a roadmap for our current and future actions. Worrying is its evil twin — destructive rather than constructive. You can worry all you want about everything that might happen in a nuclear war, but it doesn't stop it from happening.

Some worriers think they are more virtuous than those of us who aren't worrying. They believe it is irresponsible not to worry about as many things as possible. However, a life spent mulling over the worst-case scenarios to the point of distraction and insomnia is a life full of suffering. Compulsive worriers run the risk of achieving very little while missing the good stuff happening around them. As American author and Professor of Special Education at the University of Southern California Leo Buscaglia puts it: 'Worry never robs tomorrow of its sorrow, it only saps today of its joy.'

WORRYING ABOUT THE FUTURE

Our world is complex, and events regularly surprise us. We can waste a lot of time worrying about things that never happen, because we have no way of knowing for sure what *will*. You could spend years worrying about losing your partner to another person, only to lose them to cancer or a car crash — or, if you are lucky, happily grow old with them.

Terrible things will occur, that's the nature of the universe, but what those things turn out to be is harder to predict. Instead of living in torment, Seneca believed that we should back ourselves to deal with whatever arrives in the future:

> The only safe harbour in this life's tossing, troubled sea is to refuse to be bothered about what the future will bring and to stand ready and confident, squaring the breast to take without skulking or flinching whatever fortune hurls at us. —quoted on the Academy of Ideas website

You have probably faced down all sorts of problems in your life; who is to say that you won't face off the challenges to come? If the worst happens, it will happen when it happens and you will deal with it with the same resolve with which you are currently confronting the world. If you have survived up until now, you have a decent chance of coping with the future. So don't waste your brief time on this Earth worrying about it.

WORRYING ABOUT THE PAST

You can't change the past and you can't prepare for it, so why worry about it? What's gone is gone. The past is not a realm that we ever live in.

Things work best when we focus the small amount of energy we have on where we are and what we can influence. This is why the Stoics (who I'm still going on about) believed we should limit how much thinking we do about past events in our lives. That the past is only useful to teach us lessons in the hopes of bettering ourselves. You gain nothing from continually ruminating on bygones, reliving guilt.

This is not to say that we should ignore the past. Listening to The Rest is History podcast is, in my opinion, an excellent use of the present moment. Especially the eight-part series on the fall of the Aztecs. But it would be silly to work up a sweat wishing that the events depicted there had never happened. They have, and always will have. The same is true of that stupid thing you said at a party last night, the house you didn't buy that is now worth millions, or the cigarettes you smoked in your youth. It's gone; learn from it, but don't worry about it.

As I write today, my son's end-of-year exam results are due out tomorrow. I just asked him if he was worried. He looked confused. 'Nah. I studied, I'll be fine.' He's done the work and will deal with the results at the time they appear.

While your personal past creates the present and provides

information for you to use, it's important to note that your memory of it is poor. The events you look back on likely occurred differently than you remember. Memories are created in a confused, emotional way, and they change in your remembering. As Robert Wright puts it in his book *Why Buddhism is True*:

> When we recount an experience to someone, the act of recounting it changes the memory of it. So if we reshape the story a bit each time — omitting inconvenient facts, exaggerating convenient ones — we can, over time, transform our actual belief about what happened. (p. 322)

I was recently discussing on my radio show a fight that had broken out the night before on stage in Sydney between members of an American touring band. A friend of mine over in LA heard the chat on our podcast and messaged to say: 'You know those guys in that band — we partied with them over here.' I answered: 'Oh my god, I forgot. Was that the night those two dickheads were fighting outside a diner as the sun came up?' He responded: 'That was *you* fighting outside the diner as the sun came up.' One thing's for sure: one of us isn't recalling events very well.

The past is a realm that you do not exist in, you cannot influence and likely didn't happen as you remember it.

OPERATING IN THE PRESENT

Of the three realms of time, there is only one we operate in. As a matter of logic, you don't face anything 'in the future'. The struggles you encounter always occur in your present. You never reach the future because it's always 'now'. As long as events aren't happening right now, they only exist in our thoughts, and as such we aren't compelled to deal with them. *Potential* futures cause us suffering because we choose to worry about them in the present. Luckily, we have the power to stop doing this at any point.

You always have the option to ask yourself: 'How are things at this precise point in time?' The answer may be 'I am comfy in my bed', 'I am with people I love' or 'I am getting by'. Whatever happens tomorrow, you may well be in a nice place in the now; you can hold on to that, you can appreciate this moment.

Comedian Bill Burr was once asked by American entrepreneur, author and podcaster Tim Ferriss what he would most like to see written up in big letters on a billboard. Burr said he would choose the three words 'NO IT ISN'T'. In his opinion, everyone is running around claiming that all these terrible things are going to happen, so he thought it would be good to remind them: 'No it isn't.' He figures that it's better to exist in the present thinking that things are going okay, even if they turn out not to be. If bad things happen, just handle them then. Don't keep ruining right now.

We can always choose to concentrate on the things in front

of us and the people around us. I love Colin, my dog. I know dogs are around for a heartbreakingly short amount of time. I can't change that, but I can ensure my dog's time on Earth is amazing: full of walks and love and treats. It's the same with your children or anyone else in your life. You don't know what will happen, but you can aim to make whatever time there is better than it might be.

* * *

Instead of worrying about what has been, might be or what is, German philosopher Friedrich Nietzsche suggests we should resolve to love all of it. He called his formula for human greatness *amor fati*, or love fate. It's a concept that would have been familiar to Epictetus, but was used explicitly by Nietzsche in his 1908 book *Ecce Homo: How one becomes what one is*. He explains *amor fati* as wanting

> nothing to be different, not in the future, not in the past, not for all eternity. Not only to endure what is necessary, still less to conceal it . . . but to love it. (p. 1874)

In this mindset you are happy with everything that happens in life. Every moment, no matter how challenging, is to be loved. You are not just okay with the good and bad events in your life — you absolutely love all of them. *Amor fati* is about acknowledging that unfavourable things will happen, we can't stop that; but we can choose our attitude towards them, we can choose to embrace it all.

There is no point wishing things were different, so instead direct all your energies towards the way things are. Say you lose your job or your partner leaves you. That's great — you use that event as fuel. You don't focus on resentments or concerns; instead, you lean in to the change as it is now. You happily go about what you need to do. This is likely to be hard if you (say) lose your whole family in a car crash. You might not reach full *amor fati*, but aiming to love things as they are will serve you better than spending your energies on lamenting the things you can't change.

* * *

If you do choose to spend your life worrying, you could devote some of that time to worrying about what you're worrying about. You might be worrying about the wrong things. At any given moment, a lot of bad stuff is happening in the world. There are millions of things you could fret over. Some of it you are aware of, and some you are not. In the past week alone I've spent significant time worrying about social division, interest rates, government spending, rain, cancer, lice, stadium crowd numbers, the state of rugby, artificial intelligence and child literacy.

But what about all the things we haven't considered? How do we know we are worrying in the right direction? There is likely something horrific coming our way that we haven't even considered. While we ponder what we think we know, things we don't know race towards us. You could, of course, spend your days gathering as much information as you can in the hope of being across all the possibilities — but even if you successfully predict that bad thing, you still don't have the full picture. How do you know how things will turn out?

Worrying is wishing for certain outcomes over others. Yet, we will never know enough to know what events will end up creating the most positive outcomes.

In any discussion around worry, it is compulsory to bring up the famous fable of the Chinese farmer. Dr Christopher Kaczor tells the story on the website Word On Fire. A farmer and his son labour for a year with their last horse. One day, the son leaves the gate open and the horse bolts. A neighbour tells them, 'You won't be able to maintain your farm, this is terrible.' The farmer replies, 'Maybe yes, maybe no.' The next morning, the horse returns with six wild horses and the neighbour tells the farmer, 'What happiness! You can maintain the farm with two and sell the rest and make a fortune. This is great.' The farmer replies, 'Maybe yes, maybe no.' The next day the farmer's son gets thrown from one of the new horses and breaks his leg. The neighbour says, 'What a great sadness this is.' The farmer replies, 'Maybe yes, maybe no.' The next day, the army arrives to conscript all the young men in the area. They don't take the farmer's son, because of his injury. The neighbour says, 'This is great news. What a blessing!' The farmer replies, 'Maybe yes, maybe no.'

Even if the things you worry about *do* come true, you do not know whether, ultimately, it will turn out to be a good thing or a bad thing. You might be worrying about the very thing that makes life better.

* * *

As has already been mentioned, the Stoics believed that before we worry about anything, we should ask ourselves whether it is something we can control. If it is not, then worrying about it is unproductive and illogical. Our concerns will not change the outcome. Our energy would be better focused on things that our actions can actually influence.

According to Epictetus, the things we control are our beliefs, goals, judgements, values, desires and actions — how we choose to act in, and mentally position ourselves towards, the outside world. This is not to say that we shouldn't care about others. The main goal of the Stoics was to live a moral and good life in accordance with nature. In their opinion, there is nothing that can stop us from being a virtuous, joyful, trustworthy person.

For example, some people spend their time worrying about their height. This doesn't make them grow. It would be better to accept the reality of their height and use the freed-up energy to focus on areas in which they can make a difference. The serenity prayer is probably the most famous and commonly repeated expression of this dichotomy of control:

> God, grant me the serenity to accept the things I cannot change, the courage to change the things I can, and the wisdom to know the difference.

It is attributed to the German-American theologian and Christian ethicist Reinhold Niebuhr (1892–1971). Niebuhr apparently wrote it in the car as a last-minute intro to a 1932 sermon. He penned thousands of opening prayers in his life, didn't think much of this one and forgot about it completely. Luckily, a student of his, a YMCA leader called Winnifred Crane Wygal, loved it. She spotted its deeper meaning, wrote an approximation down in her journal and went on to share it across hundreds of her YMCA talks and articles. Eventually, Alcoholics Anonymous discovered it, and now it's everywhere.

It seems like a simple enough idea, but the 'wisdom to know the difference' is a little tricky. As well as the things we have complete control over, there are also things over which we have some but not complete control. Take sport. We don't have complete control over whether we win a game. That depends on a lot of factors: how good the other player is, luck, the quality of the officiating, an injury or sickness. No matter how hard you practise, you may still lose. Yet winning is not something over which you have no control at all. Practising really hard will affect your chances of winning. Therefore you have some, but not complete, control over winning a match.

It's the same with a job interview. You don't have complete control over whether you get a job, but you have a better chance of getting it if you put together a decent CV and have prepared for the interview. You do not control whether your date is going to like you or not, but you have a better chance if you have a shower, brush your teeth and put on some pants before you go.

Concentrating on doing what you can, rather than worrying about the outcome, is sometimes referred to as 'enjoying the process'. Before he was successful, *Breaking Bad* and *Malcolm in the Middle* actor Bryan Cranston was going to lots of auditions and not getting many roles. One day, he famously stopped worrying about whether he was going to get parts or not. He decided that all he could do was study the scripts, prepare, and act in the audition to the best of his ability. He gave up worrying about the decisions of those casting the roles, and instead he started enjoying the process of acting. Almost immediately, his career took off and he never looked back.

* * *

Worrying isn't just a waste of energy. It might be killing you. I zoomed David Robson, award-winning science writer and author of *The Expectation Effect: How your mindset can transform your life*, to discuss.

Me: How can worrying affect health outcomes?

Dave: The research shows very clearly that our beliefs about ageing shape our longevity. Some people see ageing as a purely negative process, and I think our culture encourages that mindset. You worry about the disability, vulnerability and cognitive decline; you expect your thinking to become less sharp. You start worrying about dementia.

All of those things create a negative mindset that has been shown to reduce lifespan by seven and a half years. It increases the risk of Alzheimer's and cardiovascular disease.

Me: That sounds crazy, how could that possibly be the case?

Dave: Well, you may exercise less if you worry that it is dangerous. If you see your body as becoming more frail all the time, you may cocoon to protect it. So there's a behavioural component; but equally profoundly, there's a direct physiological route. If you start to worry and feel more vulnerable, going to the post office or supermarket becomes more stressful. That raises the level of cortisol. After 60, suffering chronic stress leads to excessive inflammation in the body, which causes bodily wear and tear. We can even see this in the cells. The epigenetics, the gene expression, those signatures of ageing start to look older in people with this mindset. It's a faster-ticking cellular clock.

Me: What is the other option?

Dave: Other people worry less about ageing. They may see it as a time of growth. They recognise that there are ups and downs. Lots of cognitive abilities actually get better as you age. Wise reasoning improves as you get older, and your general knowledge and your vocabulary actually peaks at 70. There's a lot to look forward to, and people who accept these positive elements don't have the stress response. You see their cortisol levels declining as they get older, they're settling into old age and having a good time, and they have lower levels of inflammation and a lower risk of all of these diseases. The molecular clocks within their cells are ticking slower. They're actually biologically ageing more slowly.

The number of your age — like many other things in the world — is something you can't control. If you choose to worry about it, many of the things you are concerned about may hit you harder and earlier. Instead of worrying about the number, you could make a plan and prepare: stay active, eat healthy, get regular check-ups, spend time with others, pump some tin.

* * *

When it comes to worrying less, some people claim that these aren't normal times. That it's hard not to worry in this particular day and age, because there is just so much going on. Social division, war, climate, depression, addiction and AI. It is a commonly held belief that we live in an especially troubling time. I zoomed Tim Clare, the British author of the book *Coward*, to ask how bad we have it.

> **Me: Do you think we live in particularly worrying times?**

Tim: I don't know if this is a particularly worrying time to live. We don't have a standardised tool that we can apply across eras. But I would ask, 'When was it less worrying?' Take the 1950s. People sometimes see that as a simple *Happy Days*-style time to live. But there was polio back then. You could go to public pools and come back permanently disabled. That was an epidemic that was specifically affecting people's children. That would have been pretty worrying. The Cold War is kicking, too. Pretty worrying. The Korean War. All pretty worrying stuff.

Also, who are you imagining yourself being in these less worrying times? Probably part of a family in an American TV show in suburbia. Why are you not grieving the friends and family you lost during World War II? Why are you not in Eastern Germany? If you want me to talk about currently worrying things, I can; if you want me to talk about how stressful it was in third-century China, I can't. So do we have more to worry about now than 30, 50, 100, 1000 years ago? That's an almost impossible question to answer. But it seems unlikely things are more concerning today than they were during, say, the middle of World War II.

When you find yourself worrying about your time in history, it might be helpful to picture yourself in 536 CE, the year widely considered to be the worst in human history. Now *that* was a worrying time to be alive. It featured, among other things, war, famine and a worldwide toxic fog that turned day into night for a whole year.

In January of 536, a catastrophic Icelandic volcanic eruption spread a thick cloud of ash across most of the planet. With no volcanologists to explain what was going on, people assumed that the fog was a creation of Satan. The Byzantine historian Procopius wrote, of the event, 'A most dread evil portent took place . . . And from the time when this thing happened men were free neither from war nor pestilence nor any other thing leading to death.'

Most humans alive at the time assumed it was the end; and for many, it was. Global temperatures plummeted to a 2000-year low. Crops failed across Africa, Europe, the Middle East and Asia, and famine hit. Tens and tens of millions died, and those lucky enough to survive were hit by the Black Death five years later. Imagine the situation these people were in. They're just getting their lives back together from the satanic fog. Things are looking up. Then all of a sudden, a third of the entire global human population mysteriously drops dead in screaming pain.

536 was a terrible year in itself. But the death fog came on the back of decades and decades of horror. With the collapse of the Roman Empire in 436 CE, a lack of order had spread across Europe. Chaos and brutality, genocide, destruction, disease and starvation were standard for a century.

Our time may have its problems, but it's no 536.

NUCLEAR WASTE

We never got blown up. The nuclear winter never came. The rusty boats full of mutants never docked. All that worry — much of it manufactured by world leaders for their own ends — and the thing we feared didn't come to pass.

Sure, it could still happen — nukes and tensions still exist. Some say the chances are higher now than ever. But it hasn't happened yet. What *did* happen was decades of concern for nothing.

I didn't use that worry productively; e.g. as motivation to study global politics and then use that knowledge to go out and make a difference. I didn't even build a bunker. All I did was waste a lot of mental energy. Now I see a whole new generation of kids worrying about the end of the world. If that's you, it might be worth keeping in mind that it isn't a new or unique feeling. As Dan Carlin's book *The End is Always Near* attests, humans have had a lot to worry about forever. The best of them, however, focused their energies where it was most helpful, got on with the day to day, worked together and survived. They looked after friends, loved and brought up families — and did it all despite the endless doom and gloom.

There are always challenges ahead — personally, locally and globally. But life tends to go better when we concentrate our efforts on what we are doing now. Instead of worrying about our health, we can choose to live a healthy life and see what happens. Instead of worrying about your partner leaving you for someone else, put in the work to become a strong, fun, good person to be around, and enjoy the time you have with them. Instead of sitting around on your phone worrying about your digital addiction, take steps to curb it.

I could spend my time worrying that what I am writing here will be considered pretentious, self-helpy or a dumb piece of crap. I can't control those perceptions; I can, however, concentrate on writing to the best of my meagre abilities.

So if you don't like this book, don't worry about me. I'm not worried; I'll deal with the fallout when it comes out. :-)

Chapter Twelve

Grieving?

It's June 2023, and I'm sitting on the toilet in front of 200 people. My radio co-host Jeremy Wells and I are on stage at the Empire in central Auckland, broadcasting all day to raise awareness and money for Bowel Cancer New Zealand. This is a charity that doesn't get nearly as much attention, money and respect as it deserves. It might be because people don't like to think too much about that mucky part of the body that connects their stomach and their butt. But we really should focus on this area more. New Zealand has one of the highest rates of bowel cancer in the world. More than 3000 people are diagnosed with the disease each year, and over 1200 die. The good people at Bowel Cancer NZ need all the help they can get. Hence us being mic'd up on stage on these cold, hard bowls.

A doctor joins us on stage to discuss the grim toll the disease inflicts on our country. As she shares a particularly tragic tale about a mother in her mid-thirties leaving three children behind, it brings to mind some of the people I have lost in my life. My two best childhood friends are both gone: one was hit by a train and killed at 25, the other died of leukaemia at 32. Another good buddy took his own life a few years back, and not long after that my lovely, special mum dropped dead in her study.

I answered the phone in the middle of the night to the sound of my stunned father whispering, 'She's gone', and that was that. The most important person in the world for most of my life was no longer around. I haven't dealt sensibly with any of these passings, Mum's least of all. Now, as I look out across the crowd from my porcelain throne, it strikes me that every single person here will die. Everyone I love at home will go, too. We all will. Death is a shocking fact of life that hangs over everything we do.

Fear of the end was described by William James, the founder of American psychology, as the 'worm at the core' of human experience. There is no escaping it. If those we love don't leave us, we will leave them. Making the whole thing harder to deal with is the dark mystery of it all. We don't know when our loved ones will go; they can be taken at any time. They are here and then they are gone. It's so unreasonable. How are we supposed to deal with such a thing?

If the audience isn't enjoying watching a middle-aged man on a toilet with tears forming in his eyes they have come to the wrong place, because things are only going to get more emotional as the day goes on.

My good friend Dai Henwood, one of the funniest people

our country has ever produced, joins us. He has stage four, incurable bowel cancer. He's a fantastic, deep, caring man and he delivers the most inspirational and perspective-changing message you could ever hope to hear:

> To anyone who has received a sad diagnosis, don't sign off, mate. You are living with cancer, not dying. There is plenty of life. Every moment is something. Every day you are taking a breath, having a smile, spending time with the people you love — you are living, and it's actually the same for everyone, sick or not. Please just enjoy what you have, while you have it, with the people you love. We all have some life to live.

Such courage, such hope — the venue explodes into spontaneous applause. Dai jokes with me afterwards: 'I've never seen *you* get a standing ovation for talking on the radio.'

* * *

When C.S. Lewis, author of the 100-million-selling *Chronicles of Narnia* series, lost his wife, Joy, to cancer, he slid into a deep despair — which he documented across four notebooks that were later compiled into the book *A Grief Observed* and published under the pseudonym N.W. Clerk. It's a deeply personal, and from my experience extremely accurate, account of what grief does to us. The book was so good that friends of Lewis, not knowing he had written it, recommended it to him to deal with his loss. In it Lewis talks about feeling slightly drunk or concussed after his wife died. He felt separated from the world, like he was walking around under an invisible blanket. The words of others were hard to take in; set against the weight of his grief, they seemed uninteresting to him. Yet he didn't want to be alone; he dreaded being in an empty house. Lewis wanted lots of people around, just not talking directly at him.

Grief can be both a mental and a physiological experience. You want the person you love back so badly that it physically hurts. You clench your fists. Stress hormones course through your body. It's primal. Lewis described it as an 'amputation'.

After my dad told me that my lovely mum had died, I sat in silence by myself in the dark for a few minutes. Then, suddenly, I stood up, yelled, and tipped over every chair and table in the room. I kicked walls and consumed all the alcohol I could find. The mother of my children found me the next morning in the most clichéd of grief poses, passed out face-down in the middle of the lounge with an empty bottle of Jack Daniel's beside me. Mum's passing drove me crazy that night, partly because I was at the other end of the country from her and there was nothing I could do. It's safe to say that my insane, destructive, drunken behaviour didn't help me or anyone else.

In a 2020 article for The Conversation, John Frederick Wilson, Director of Bereavement Services Counselling at York

St John University, discusses what happens in real time in the brain when we are grieving.

> In MRI scans, a brain region called the nucleus accumbens, which lights up when we talk fondly of our loved ones, also glows at our grief at losing them.

It would appear that grief occurs in the same brain space as love.

* * *

Our ancestors needed each other around, so we developed emotions that strengthened our bonds. Just like the feelings of love and of loneliness, grief is all about keeping us together. Evolutionary biologists believe that the aggressive first stages of grief developed to motivate us to search for our lost ones. The hurt we feel when people are taken away drives us to attempt to get them back any way we can.

The primitive parts of our brain don't know if we'll be able to find or help the lost person. It just compels us to frantically act on the off-chance we can. When there is no productive action to take, we may scream in agony and (in my case) smash and drink things. This initial feeling of loss is similar to the panicked feeling that parents experience when their two-year-old runs off in the supermarket. We go crazy looking for them. A madness takes over: we rush around in a craze, yelling their name in complete strangers' faces, only to find the child two rows over happily staring at the lollies.

In the case of a deceased loved one, over time we usually find acceptance and the aggressive protesting stage passes. We move into a more passive despair. This change encourages us to stop expending energy on directly searching, fighting, screaming and grasping for the person, and instead attempt a return to normal activities. Unfortunately, grief is such a powerful emotion that when we begin to come to terms with our loss, we often don't want to. C.S. Lewis talks about how feeling better over Joy came with a shot of shame. He felt obligated to prolong his unhappiness in order to honour her memory.

Over time, however, we do come to terms with a loss and can start to put our efforts into reconnecting with others. In the case of a lost partner, we may allow ourselves to search for a new one. Death, as bad as it is, can encourage us to form new bonds and strengthen old ones. It can bring those who are left behind together in the shared identity of the loss. Like most things we humans do, grief is all about our connections with each other.

SAYING GOODBYE

When a loved one dies, you can try to find solace in the shared experience of it all. You can tell yourself that you'll feel better one day, that death is a part of life, and that you were lucky to have the time you did with the person you loved, but these logical concepts don't help as much as they should. Reason and rationality can be hard to come by in times of loss.

In 1969, Elisabeth Kübler-Ross changed how many in the Western world think about grieving with her book *On Death and Dying*. She created the now-famous five stages of grief: denial, anger, bargaining, depression and acceptance. These steps came to be known as the Kübler-Ross model, and have been widely used to describe the grieving process ever since.

These ideas are so well known that in the middle of grief, we tend to wonder which phase we are currently in and how quickly we'll arrive at the final one: acceptance. 'If I can just get through the five stages, I'll be cured.' Sadly, this is not the case. The Kübler-Ross model was never meant to be applied to grieving a lost one. Elizabeth was analysing people dealing with their own death after being diagnosed with a terminal illness. *Not* the loss of someone else.

In her book *The Truth About Grief: The myth of its five stages and the new science of loss*, Ruth Davis Konigsberg challenges the universality, helpfulness and validity of Kübler-Ross's model. Konigsberg believes that grief is a very complex and individual experience, and we simply do not go through the five stages in an orderly, linear manner. The bereaved tend to jump all over the place. We may feel acceptance one day, then jump right back to anger, then to depression, and then back again. Noticing that you're feeling depressed about the situation doesn't mean you're one step away from acceptance and out the other side. You may well go back into denial, or any of the other emotions that circle around grieving.

Equally, those observing a grieving person can't make any assumptions about how the subject is progressing. Just because your grieving friend is currently 'bargaining', it doesn't mean they are about to get depressed. On the contrary, Konigsberg encourages the bereaved to accept their grieving process as unique to them. She believes we should reject pressure to fit into anyone else's set stages. We should attempt to be compassionate with ourselves. Reach out to friends, family and professionals if we feel the need, while allowing ourselves our own timeframe to work through things. There is, in her opinion, no right or wrong way to go about it. She feels that instead of pressuring ourselves to overcome our grief, or pushing ourselves towards acceptance, we should try to integrate the loss into our lives as we go. To honour the memory of our lost loved ones while still moving forward with life the best we can.

As usual, the Stoic philosophers looked at things in a more direct manner. In 49 CE, Lucius Annaeus Seneca wrote an essay for his father-in-law Paulinus entitled *De Brevitate Vitae (On the Shortness of Life)* after he lost a loved one. In it Seneca argued that we should face our grief head-on. That it is more beneficial to overcome sorrow than to try to mask it. If we put our efforts into distracting ourselves with pleasures, inebriation and distraction, it's likely that the pain will keep returning until we are forced to face it. It can keep damaging us for years and years if we don't stare it in the eye right away.

Seneca told his father in-law that he would not prescribe remedies or practices such as taking up new activities to deal with the grief, because he believed it was better to bring feelings to a head now rather than try to distract oneself from them.

It seems to me that tangihanga takes a somewhat head-on approach to grief. When someone on their mother's side of the family passes, my kids will spend three days staying at the marae with the deceased there in an open coffin. The departed will be acknowledged at many gatherings to come; but after days at the marae sleeping, eating and playing around your lost relation's body, there is no hiding from the fact that this beloved person has passed on.

* * *

It's not only other people's deaths that can cause us to grieve. Our powerful human desire for connection creates a problem when we contemplate our own end. Our death will inevitably separate us from our loved ones. It removes us from our future on Earth and our future with others.

Neurosurgeon Paul Kalanithi was diagnosed with inoperable lung cancer at the age of 36. In his last year of life he wrote the brilliant, posthumously published *When Breath Becomes Air*. It's an awe-inspiring book that I recommend whether you are dealing with grief or not. After his diagnosis, his wife, Lucy, asked him what part of death concerned him the most. Paul told her that it was leaving her. From his perspective, his death was not just the loss of his life but a brutal separation from his beloved wife. During his sickness, he and Lucy brought baby Cady into the world. This gifted Paul eight months of parental joy — but it also complicated his departure further. To him, his death meant losing his family. In his book, Paul outlines the enormity of the problem we mortals face. His whole life, he had been building towards something meaningful. Now, all of that would go unrealised. His hard-won future did not exist. Kalanithi had dealt with death many times before with his patients, and thought his experience with this might show him the way. But it didn't. Paul's future would be up to other people to live.

The epilogue of *When Breath Becomes Air* was written by Lucy after Paul had gone. It's about as heart-breaking and powerful a thing as you could ever hope to read. From within her grief, she honours the person he was. She expected to be heartbroken by his passing, but didn't anticipate that she would continue to love him just the same. On top of terrible, heavy sorrow, she also felt gratitude towards him for what he had achieved.

> I miss him acutely nearly every moment, but I somehow feel I'm still taking part in the life we created together. (p. 146)

On the surface, the fact that we all die seems inescapably grim; like a shadow that falls across our entire lives. We spend our time consciously trying not to die but knowing that eventually we will. Yet, counter-intuitively, many philosophers argue that our finitude is a positive thing. That far from fearing death, we should embrace it. That we can use our coming demise as the inspiration to live.

* * *

In *Four Thousand Weeks: Time management for mortals*, Oliver Burkeman argues that accepting our own death leads to a more fulfilling life. He points out if we live to 80, we only get 4000 weeks. If you're reading this, you'll have eaten up a bunch of time already. You may recoil in horror at the shortness of life, but it won't change it. We can tinker around the edges, gain years here and there, but there is nothing we can do to stop the end from coming. It may come tomorrow.

Burkeman argues that accepting this limited time can motivate us to appreciate what we have and to pick worthwhile things to do with it. No matter how many productivity books we read, life hacks we employ or apps we download, we will never generate enough time to experience everything available on planet Earth. Having your funeral firmly in mind might motivate you to choose what you do carefully. To use what time you have wisely.

I zoom Oliver at his UK home, to discuss death and the proper usage of our remaining time. Ironically my call takes him away from the lovely family BBQ I can see going on in the background.

Me: Oliver, you point out that we have a very short time on Earth. Why should we stop running away from that terrifying fact and instead lean in to it?

Oliver: The tough-love response to that question is, like it or not, that's the way it is. It's not being a finite human that's the problem. It's the conviction that there must be some way around this situation. There isn't. You could instead feel grateful that you have any time at all. I believe that if we face our finitude, we can value our time and cultivate a fulfilling life.

Me: What should we do with our time?

Oliver: Haha, well, there's no effective limit to the number of things we could possibly do with the time we have. If you attempt to do it all, you're not gonna get around to the things that actually matter to you. I don't think it's helpful, or my job, to list what people should do with their lives. I just hope to clear the fog a little bit. Help people see their time differently.

> Having said that, one of the things I love to mention is from James Hollis, the psychotherapist: he suggests you ask yourself whether a given path or choice in life enlarges you or diminishes you. It doesn't work for everybody, but many people, including myself, find that a powerful way to connect to something intuitively. That sense of does this choice enlarge me? You usually know on some unspoken level if it does. That's a good way to distinguish between options in the time you have, but I totally refuse to give the list of things that you should be doing with your limited time here. That's up to you.

If we remind ourselves how short life is, we might stop wasting time on trivial things. We will ask ourselves questions around our usage of the few moments we have. 'Is this petty argument worth the time it's taking up?', 'Does this average TV series deserve this chunk of my existence?', 'Do I really want to waste my precious years on Earth complaining, angry, worried, lonely, greedy, annoyed or offended?' With our eye on our mortality, every second we have becomes precious. Find a way to feel grateful for the time we have, and we can honour our lives by doing worthwhile things.

From another perspective, but with death still in mind, even the mundane things we do can have meaning. Everything we do, we will one day do for the last time. The next time might be it. Concentrating on this could be seen as morbid, but you could also see it as inspiring. It invests a special significance in everything we do. It's like the last dinner with a lover who is going overseas. You've had dinner together many times, but because it's now the last time it means so much more.

In *When Breath Becomes Air*, with his terminal disease getting worse, Kalanithi writes about the last surgery he performed. As he arrived at the hospital, he became keenly aware of everything like never before. He had parked in the same spot thousands of times before, but as he stepped out of his car in the early hours of the morning, he noticed pleasant eucalyptus and pine fragrances for the first time. This previously meaningless sensation was suddenly everything.

In the Japanese form of Zen Buddhism, the concept of *mono no aware* (the pathos of things) teaches that if we keep in mind that everything will die, we are reminded to appreciate things while they are around. Cherry blossom is central to the understanding of this concept. The flowers of the cherry tree exist in their full glory for just a couple of days. This delicate brevity makes their beauty all the more intense and meaningful.

This meaningful scarcity is present for our whole lives, if we look for it. Everyone and everything is going away soon. You may enjoy your time at a job more if you acknowledge that today could be the last day. The same is true of your commute, brushing your teeth, eating a pie, walking to the shops, cooking and breathing. You will appreciate your children more when you keep in mind that they'll move out soon and you will see them less and less. One day you will see them for the last time. If your parents currently live in another city, you may only see them another half-dozen times before they go. It's worth savouring every one of those visits. This view of life with death at the forefront can make everything you have precious.

* * *

Life may be short but it may also be long enough. Seneca argues that nature gives us plenty of time to accomplish great things, and that life only seems short because we waste the time we have. A life of mindless repetition and easy options flies by, while a life packed with variety, learning, loving and other meaningful experiences is plenty long enough.

In July 2023 I experience a superficial but stark example of the choice we have. There is a FIFA World Cup game being played at Eden Park Stadium at the end of my street. I could have bought tickets, I could have attended with my friends and family. I could have experienced a once-in-a-lifetime event. Instead, I sit at the same pub I always go to, telling the same friends the same stories I always tell. Which was, as usual, a lot of fun — but we could have chosen to up sticks and witness history 400 metres away instead of sitting where we always sit and drinking until we hardly knew where we were. That day could have been significant, a noteworthy experience. Instead it raced by, in the same way as many others, not worth registering as an event at all.

In the 2004 movie *Shaun of the Dead*, we see Londoners walking around, living their lives, in such a zoned-out zombie-like state that it takes Shaun a long time to notice that the apocalypse has actually come. The living don't act differently enough from the undead for him to register the change. Are we afraid of dying because we are going to miss more time staring into our phones, passing out drunk, mindlessly piling junk food into our faces, watching rubbish TV in silence? Many of us spend our lives fearing death while indulging in the very activities that disrespect the time we have, physically shortening it and speeding it up in our minds.

* * *

After my lovely mum died, I did exactly what Seneca advises against. I refused to accept it. I wilfully hid from the situation. I put all photos of her away, hid all the wonderful birthday cards and books she had hand-made me and the kids in a box, deleted her number from my phone so I wouldn't see it as I scrolled through. I refused to look at texts or emails that people sent me if they referred to her. I completely shut out anything that could remind me of Mum. I refused to discuss the topic with friends or loved ones. Refused to look at her in her coffin at the funeral. If the mother of my children attempted to bring her up in conversation, I would leave the room. It just hurt too much.

But despite my cowardly attempts to ignore reality, I couldn't stop Mum from appearing in my dreams. I'd wake up happy, thinking that she was still around, only to remember again and again that she wasn't. Each time it was like I was hearing the sad news for the first time. All my hiding didn't stop me reaching for the phone to ring her whenever anything good happened in my life, either.

My father, Christopher, was not in a position to hide from our tragic situation; he was forced to experience it head-on. At the time of her death he had been happily married to my mum for nearly 50 years. One evening, he was working at his desk when a show they planned to watch together came on. Dad wondered why she hadn't come down to the lounge and went to look for her. He found her lying on the floor in her study. Being medically trained, he immediately knew she was dead, but he performed CPR anyway. Mum had had some health issues, but this was a complete shock. The house filled with police and ambulance staff. Dad described himself as feeling detached and in control, throughout, but later realised that he'd given the police their wedding anniversary date not her birth date. I recently talked to him about it over several shots of his favourite whisky.

Me: So, Dad, can you describe the first few days after we lost Mum?

Dad: My family did not leave me alone and I was grateful for that, although I had no plans to follow her. My training left me no escape into denial — I recall a powerful feeling of self-pity. What is to happen to me now I have lost this person who has been the cornerstone of my adult years and who I loved beyond defining? I was well informed about the theories of death, dying and grieving, and nowhere had I seen mention of self-pity as part of grieving; yet, it seems to me, it is not an unnatural response.

I was also desperately concerned that she had died alone. Had she tried to call out? Was she aware of what was happening to her? If only she had died in the same room — I could have held her while she died and could have said goodbye and reaffirmed my love. Later, the postmortem and the report for the Coroner reassured me that the cause of her death was one of the very few medical conditions where death is near to instantaneous, so I take great comfort in the thought that she was unconscious before she hit the floor.

Me: She was such a huge part of your life, how did you go about rebuilding?

Dad: I was blessed because I could talk to my students about the process I was going through and the medical aspects of her death. This was a real-life experience which might be of use to them in the future. I am glad because after the initial few weeks, no one outside my immediate family and friends wanted to talk with me about my grieving. I was lucky because my family were so close and supportive while struggling to come to terms with their own loss in their own ways. Since then, I have found new activities to help me rebuild. I left our house and farm of 35 years very quickly because I was overwhelmed with memories of our special lifestyle in that setting and because I did not want to continue that without her. I began reading anything I could find on grieving.

Me: Did you learn anything surprising about grief?

Dad: That the stages elaborated by Kübler-Ross are of no relevance in grieving whatsoever. Each death has its own unique circumstances. Too often, well-meaning acquaintances seem to expect progress through defined stages. I was forthright about this with my students in the hope that they would not impose such concepts on their grieving patients.

Me: How are you now, Dad?

Dad: I am an old man, so my thoughts are inclined to focus on the past and they are mostly very happy. My time with your mother over all those years is inextricably entwined with my memories and I am very happy to be there. I still

> wear a wedding ring, which seems to be a vexed question in our society — not that anyone has ever asked me about why I persist. It is simple: I still feel happily married, and the ring is a tangible link to her and our time together. And, I suspect, I feel I have been so fortunate in my relationship with her and with the precious family we produced that I have no need whatsoever to seek to replicate any part of that with anyone else. She will always be in my thoughts — and that is not a meaningless cliché!

LOVE YOU, MUM

We aren't around for long, and nor are the ones we love. Some people have a lot less time than you, and some have a lot more. If we are lucky, we get enough time to experience many different things; and if we are even luckier, we get to share them with others. We will spend a chunk of our time here grieving for those we love and lose. How we face those losses is up to us; what we *don't* want to do is waste our lives grieving for ourselves or, worse, being so ungrateful for the life we have that we don't bother to live it.

In the movie *Gladiator*, Marcus Aurelius (played by Richard Harris) tells Maximus (Russell Crowe) that:

> Death smiles at us all. All a man can do is smile back.

The real Marcus didn't actually say this, but it is still an awesome thought. Death is coming for all of us, and there is nothing we can do about it. We can, however, accept that fact, look it in the eye, smile about it and choose to use the time we have wisely.

I remember the last phone call I had with my lovely mum *so* clearly. It was a typical conversation between us. A long, philosophical, sometimes heated discussion about life. Eventually she had to go. The last words I said to her were 'Love you, Mum.' Across my lifetime we spoke millions of words to each other, and those were the last three. I'm happy that I got another 'Love you, Mum' in before she went.

Chapter Thirteen

Aimless?

We are expecting our first child. For a year or two now, my life has lacked direction. My dreams don't seem to be coming true and I'm not sure what I'm supposed to be doing next.

This incoming life gives us something to focus on. We name our boy in advance, place a calendar on the wall and count down the days till Charlie will bless us with his presence. It's exciting and terrifying at the same time. So much so that on the crucial surprise arrival night I get completely steamed and, much to my shame, am in no state to help.

Luckily, Charlie's mother is incredibly onto it. She is, and always has been, instantly brilliant at everything she attempts, and preparing for a baby was no different. Whereas I have been a liability throughout the whole build-up, she has taken responsibility and organised every single detail. Thanks to her, we have met with our midwife multiple times, saved up for and purchased the right pram, cot and car seat. She has booked the birth in at the hospital, and after-birth care, every blanket and all necessary items of clothing await our incoming wee boy. We have even attended several boring two-hour prenatal classes (which I fell asleep in).

No thanks to this loser here, everything is under control.

Then it all goes horribly wrong. Charlie is a massive baby, and after many hours of brave pushing at the hospital things are not progressing. I spend the time feeling shocked at the painful nature of human birthing, guilty over how easy I have it in comparison to her, and completely wasted from sucking on the nitrous.

Eventually it is decided that a C-section is required. Everything is readied and we are about to head through to surgery when an emergency birth comes piling into the hospital. Our baby is currently safe and healthy, so we are put on hold. Then another emergency comes through and we are put on hold again. Then another critical non-booked birth is put before ours. Now all of a sudden Charlie needs to come out immediately and the unprecedented amount of emergency birthing traffic is preventing that from happening.

Things are getting stressful and I am no help at all. There is nowhere good for me to stand. Medical people are yelling 'She has to go in NOW!!!' I couldn't agree more. This is out of control. Finally we are moved through to surgery, but the anaesthetic isn't doing its job. After several injections, mum can still feel everything. Again there is nothing I can do to help.

The theatre staff start arguing. I ask frantic questions, but no one answers. The anaesthetist screams at a doctor and throws a drip bag and stand across the theatre. It's like a TV medical drama. It's terrifying. I yell 'What the hell is going on here?' and am pushed out into the corridor. Of course I can't handle it out there, I need to know what's happening, so I sneak in through a side room to peer in through the door. They have no choice but to give her a general anaesthetic. She is now out cold.

A C-section is a brutal thing, hard to comprehend — but finally, thankfully, Charlie is here. A second of sweet relief . . . then a horrible shock: he isn't breathing. People are panicking again. Charlie is turning blue. I am on my knees in the strange side resource room begging for someone or something to save him. There is mad commotion in the theatre. I jump up and push my way in. A nurse tells me 'You can't be in here', but I don't care. I have to be. All hope seems lost. I can't believe we are going to lose our little boy. Someone who I have only seen through a window and his mum hasn't seen at all.

Then — suddenly, thankfully — it all goes beautifully well. They unblock Charlie's throat and colour quickly returns to his face. I experience levels of joy and relief the likes of which I have never felt. Moments later, I am holding this little miracle. The first time I have held any baby in my life. His brave mum is still unconscious, and with the amount of drugs they've pumped into her she will be for a while. It's just me and him for now.

That's when things get really scary. I know absolutely

nothing about parenting, thanks to snoozing through baby classes, and pester the nurse with incredibly stupid questions. Like, 'Will he just keep breathing on his own or do I have to do something?' They hand me a bottle, and the little trooper gets stuck right in and drains it all. Starting a lifelong love of rapidly consuming and spilling drinks.

In the first moments holding my first-born son — looking at him, my heart bursting with pride and gratitude to his mum for making him — my mission in life becomes clear. I need to sort my crap out, stop being such a loser and start earning enough to look after this guy and his mother. I need to quit pissing around following undefined dreams, drinking, partying and being a selfish prick. I need to get a real job so I can buy these two a house to live in. That is my purpose.

At this point it is a big ask, and I will continue to fail and fall short of this pledge regularly for a long time afterwards; but it is nice to finally have a direction in life. My existence is no longer aimless, and I feel great. Which is odd: why would looking down the barrel at years of hard work for the good of someone else bring so much relief?

* * *

The Experience Machine is a thought experiment first outlined by American philosopher Robert Nozick in his 1974 book *Anarchy, State, and Utopia*.

The idea goes something like this. There's a complete mental immersion device that you can be plugged into for the rest of your life. When you are connected, everything seems completely real and you don't know you are in there. Before you enter the machine, you get to choose the experiences you want. You would likely choose all the most positive things you can think of. Everything you desire. Wealth, love, beauty, sexual gratification, fame, sporting prowess, successful kids and a rocking bod. Once attached, your biological requirements are provided for, and you experience all the pleasure you could ever want for the rest of your life.

Nozick's question was this: if offered the choice to be attached to the Experience Machine and live the remainder of your life pleasured and satisfied, would you? It turns out, probably not.

A 2014 study by Dan Weijers from Victoria University of Wellington found that 84% of people asked to contemplate this choice said they wouldn't plug in. Pleasure like this seems meaningless to most of us. We value wrestling with reality. We want our lives to have some point above mainlined happiness. We want the people we love to be real. Having it handed to us seems too easy.

It reminds me of a heroin-using friend of mine I watched over many years. One day I found him standing with eyes closed, swaying from side to side, in my hallway. There was a needle hanging out of his arm and blood from his stuck vein was splattered on the walls. Lost in his drug-addled world, he had a lovely, contented smile on his face. He looked very happy indeed — but I didn't want to be him. I also didn't want to clean up his blood and vomit. The next day, he didn't want to be himself either.

When Nozick came up with his idea 50 years ago, it was a science-fiction impossibility, invoked purely to make a point. Nowadays, developments in virtual reality make the whole thing seem very possible. But if we don't want to plug in to some virtual reality machine, how do we find meaning in the real world?

* * *

In a hunter-gatherer society, you had to prove your worth to your clan in ways we don't nowadays. Everyone's lives depended on individuals doing their bit. Meaning came from your family surviving. Your path was clear and your success quantifiable. At the end of each day you could sit in front of the campfire and feel strong satisfaction that you had made it through. If you and your family were still alive, you were succeeding.

This powerful but simple meaning is missing from most of our lives. 'The people I love not getting eaten today' is a more easily defined Key Performance Indicator than 'Am I rich, famous and hot yet?'

Prehistoric humans learned from their elders and worked hard to perfect the needed skills. Competency earned them a place and a purpose. You could become the best in your tribe at something valuable; find a way to contribute in a very real life-or-death way. Our ancestors scanned the forest floor for things to eat so they could survive. Today we scroll through streaming platforms, unable to decide on anything to watch. Back then, your satisfaction in life came from doing your bit for the 30 people you knew intimately and cared about dearly. Contributing to keeping everyone alive provided you with a varied and rewarding existence. It would have been hard, terrifying and violent on occasion, and sickness, superstition or starvation could take you down at any time. But it would all have felt very meaningful.

Nowadays, for many of us, our biggest challenge in life is getting to bed without stuffing so much food, entertainment and booze in our heads that we have to get up three times in the night. It's a given that you will have enough to survive; the trick is not eating so much that you die at 55. There are so many options, potential callings in life and directions we can go in that most of us can't make a choice. The term 'I don't know what to do with my life' is bandied about from around age fifteen until we give up on everything at 45. As Tyler Durden states in Chuck Palahniuk's novel *Fight Club*: 'We are raised by television to believe that someday we'll be millionaires and movie stars and rock stars, but we won't. And we're just learning this fact.'

These days it's much harder to impress yourself and others with your skills. We can go online and watch someone better than us at everything we could want to do. As a result, many of us live with the sinking feeling that we don't contribute anything important to our — or anyone else's — life. As William B. Irvine put it in our Zoom call:

> You've got eight billion people that you can go online and try to impress. To compare yourself to. We've outgrown our wiring, but the problem is the wiring is still there. It's not going to change. So we have to do our best to learn, to live with it.

With all the success we see on social media, an honourable, hard-working life doesn't feel like enough. We crave meaning, but we don't know where to find it. We walk around feeling like there are important and fulfilling things we should be doing but we're not sure what they are. So we end up doing the easy things that we know are the exact opposite of meaningful.

Something isn't right. What is it that's missing from our lives?

WE NEED FRICTION

The effort, struggle, complexity and obstacles of our existence can be described as friction. If we don't have anything to rub up against, we don't grow and we don't experience the satisfaction that comes with that. It's like lifting weights to build muscles. This friction might be the very thing that brings us meaning in life. As JFK stated in his famous 1962 address on man going to the moon: '[We do these things] not because they are easy, but because they are hard.' The age we live in is comfortable and getting more so each day. Big tech is constantly seeking out frictions to smooth out. If they zero in on an area and find a way to remove it, they make *billions*.

Friction in the use of taxis led to the creation of Uber; the effort needed to go to the shops brings us Amazon; removing the difficulty in finding information makes Google its money. There was friction in renting DVDs, now streaming puts it all at our fingertips. There is no walking down to the store and interacting with a potential Quentin Tarantino behind the counter anymore. With the prod of a single finger, we can get all the movies in the world.

While tech companies are removing the effort we need to put in to get what we want, they're also removing the human contact. Arguably the thing that brings us the most meaning in life. Online pornography removes the complexities of reckoning with other people, but few would say it is as meaningful as time spent with a real person.

Josh Homme is the vocalist and guitarist of the hugely successful American rock band Queens of the Stone Age. In 2024, this tall, talented and good-looking man discussed his views on technology, friction and human interaction with me and my co-host Jeremy Wells on *The Matt & Jerry Show* on Radio Hauraki.

Me: To form a band, you need to find someone to play drums; you need to convince a friend to become a bass player. You have to get a band room and practice in it. It's difficult. Nowadays, most kids have the technology at their fingertips that allows them to digitally record every part of a band in their rooms at home by themselves. Tech has made it easier to do on your own, but what do you think is lost when you take other people out of making music?

Josh: For me, the relationships that go into the creative process are an education in how you live your life. How do you collaborate? Do you dominate, do you belittle someone to get your ideas across, or do you support somebody? In the end, you get something that's been filtered through multiple people's brains and interpretations. It's gorgeous.

I think things can sometimes become too perfected, too quantised and too streamlined. Perfection is an ideal you strive for together but would never want to achieve because perfection sounds boring. There's no collision. There's no rub. If you play a viola, you take a bow, rub it on the strings, and it's all about the friction. In music, as you stack things, you want the rub. Music that is perfect seems safe to me because no one is colliding in it. No one backs their car into anyone else in the making of it. Like everything, it's about friction. I think about the universe

> being made in friction from the collision of things. I think of babies being made in friction. I think of relationships being made in friction and music being made in friction. When I am making music, I look at the value of borrowing friction from others.

In *A Book of Secrets*, Derren Brown points out the many unforeseen consequences of friction removal. One example he discusses is the 'Like' button on Facebook. This was introduced to make it easier to express an opinion. To make communication smoother. No need to spend the time to compose a response — just click. But it created a monster. A worldwide obsession grew from the desire to gain social media 'likes' and 'follows', and this has led to desperate attention-seeking behaviour. Humans are spending more and more time and energy trying to collect these meaningless ticks of approval that still leave them feeling hollow and wanting more. Controversial, nonsensical and enraging opinions are encouraged because they attract more engagement.

The lust for likes has generated more and more anger and division. Most of us would agree that this isn't a healthy way to spend the precious moments of our lives. It is, however, low-effort — as is ordering food with an app. Eating out involves leaving the house, and interacting with wait-staff, other customers and the person or people you are with. Clicking a few icons on your phone is way less effort. But taken to the extreme, the least frictionless way to feed would be intravenously in your sleep.

An automated needle attached to your bed could find a vein and pump sustenance right in. Efficient, but not very human or meaningful.

This contrasts with the Japanese tea ceremony, known as *chanoyu* or *sadō*. Every part of the process is carried out mindfully. The tea space is prepared and the essential equipment is carefully laid out. Teapot, cups, whisk, scoop, and finally towels. Each utensil is then mindfully cleansed in hot water, which is subsequently discarded. The tea leaves are carefully scooped into the teapot, followed by the slow addition of hot water, and then stirred. The tea is allowed to steep for many minutes before it is poured. When the drinking time arrives, it is also done mindfully. You savour the flavour and aroma. Experience all the sensory elements in silent reflection and inner peace. A cup of tea has become meaningful through added friction.

We live in a world where obtaining the food we need to survive can be achieved with no physical effort or human contact. It's easy in the short term, but we all know that this is not as meaningful as taking the time to prepare a quality meal for friends or family and then sitting down to eat it with them. There will be complex interactions, dozens of decisions, work and pressure — but also laughs, bonding, and ultimately satisfaction and meaning.

In our Zoom call I asked Oliver Burkeman about the meaning of friction and effort in life.

Me: What does the march towards efficiency mean for humans?

Oliver: It's an interesting question. If you take anything to its ultimate level of efficiency, all sorts of things become meaningless. I write about hiking in the country. Obviously, the most efficient way to get from the start point to the end point when you're walking in a loop is not to start in the first place. But that is not a meaningful walk. The effort of doing it, the walking, the people you are with, the experience – that is meaningful. More and more, we are being sold less human contact to make things work better. Less effort to get things. It may seem easier at the time, but be wrong in terms of your deeper need to belong to a community.

We are pretty bad at understanding what it is that makes us happy. As a result, we're too ready to get rid of things that feel like irritations when these seemingly more difficult things are the very things that give us meaning in life and actually make us happy.

Maybe it's a solid day in the office; maybe building a shed, writing a song, or organising a massive out-of-control hen party. Whatever it is, we tend not to feel aimless in life when we welcome friction by taking on difficult tasks.

While driving by a building site years ago on a windy, rainy day, I said to my son: 'Looks cold up there.' He replied, 'Yeah, but it would be so awesome when you get home knowing you built something today, then you're all warm and then dinner would taste so good.' Pretty smart for a nine-year-old.

When we take on a difficult task with others, that's when a sense of purpose really kicks in. Doing things with a team 'not because they are easy, but because they are hard' is what humans were born to do. Of course, you can work too much.

THE PROBLEM WITH WORK

Not all effort and friction is healthy. Closer to the end of their days, some people feel like they wasted their lives on one particularly time-consuming part of it.

Paul Tsongas was a US Senator for Massachusetts. In 1983 he was diagnosed with cancer and decided to re-evaluate his life choices. He chose to quit his job. In 1984 he published the memoir *Heading Home*, which included this now much-heard line:

> No one on his deathbed ever said, 'I wish I had spent more time on my business.' (p. 159)

It is often misquoted, with 'at work' or 'at the office' replacing 'on my business', but the point it makes remains the same: we can spend too much time at work, to the detriment of other meaningful things in our lives. That's all very well, but most of us have no choice but to work a lot. Little work means little money and an extremely stressful life, potentially living on the street.

Apart from a few high-level Zen Buddhists who may find peace from within with nothing, we need to find a way to make money and work compatible with happiness. As American neuroscientist Dr Andrew D. Huberman points out in his podcast, 'it's a little naive to assume that somehow, work is counter to happiness'. While money doesn't determine happiness, if you work and also manage to spend some money on the right things, then it might help. Maybe you get to do recreational things you enjoy. Maybe you spend on things that create a social connection. Money definitely releases stress around healthcare and education in a family.

And work isn't just work. A lot of the other special things you need in life occur at your job. These are places full of social interactions. How many people meet their lovers in the office, or steamed at work parties? How many good friends do we make on-site? We bond over hard work, then celebrate a job well done.

Still, there is no doubt that some of us work too much, myself included. We end up neglecting family, friends and fitness. As the cliché goes, it's a balance — or is it?

Professor Scott Galloway is a hugely successful businessman who teaches that balance is a myth, especially when you're young. He believes the happy family life he has now was set up by working insanely hard as a young man. I zoom the prof at his beautiful Florida mansion and talk work while he lies back in a deck chair by an impressive-sized pool. He tells me:

> Capitalist societies are forgiving places for people with money, and harsh rapacious places for people without. Few people develop economic security without working their asses off for 10 to 20 years. It cost me my hair, my first marriage, and it was worth it because now I can take the afternoon and watch my son play rugby. It's not because I'm a great dad. It's because I was very focused on my career and I got lucky, too.
>
> That was my way. That's not to say that's the right way. Some people decide at an earlier age they don't want to live to work. They move to a lower-cost area, live a modest lifestyle and spend more time with family and friends their entire life. If they're making connections, great. I respect that. But I tell young people, turn off the Hallmark version of work and life, where we can maintain our career, relationships, donate time, make a ton of money and coach little league. Be clear there is no such thing as balance. There are just trade-offs.

The question is, how much do you want to sacrifice? Scott Galloway also points out that professional achievement isn't very meaningful if you have no one to share it with. In his book *The Algebra of Happiness*, he writes that with the right partner, the fruits of your hard work feel real. It connects what you do back to your species: you are once again working for your tribe.

ANOTHER PATH — GRATITUDE

The word 'gratitude' gets bandied about so much these days it can feel a little trite to use it, but we shouldn't let that stop us. If you are looking to enjoy your life it's an important quality to foster, and as such it deserves to be discussed. I for one am grateful for the word. I also feel grateful to the lovely American woman who taught me how to be thankful in 2017, when I was lucky enough to spend Thanksgiving holiday at the historic Peabody Hotel in Memphis. It's a fancy old establishment famous for keeping ducks in a castle-like 'Duck Palace' on the roof. They've done this since 1933. Each day a Duck Master in a red coat and tails marches the flock into a special lift, across a specially laid red carpet and into the fountain in the lobby. They swim there all day, and then in the afternoon he marches them back home. It's the greatest example of injecting meaning into something meaningless that I have ever seen.

On Thanksgiving Day, my four Kiwi friends and I stuff our faces for three straight hours at the Peabody's palatial restaurant. The largest spread of food I have ever encountered. None of us has ever been so full. Our waitress is a big-boned, no-nonsense southerner in her sixties. During my second bottle of red, I ask her: 'What are we supposed to do on Thanksgiving?' She whacks me playfully round the head with a napkin and tells me 'Don't be silly', before backing away laughing and shaking her head. She can't comprehend that anyone wouldn't know.

When she comes back I ask again: 'Seriously, we're from

New Zealand — we don't celebrate Thanksgiving. What do we do? Do we give presents, do I do a speech, what do we do?' She laughs and hits me round the head again. 'You just think about what you are grateful for and then maybe tell people.' I joke 'But I am full of resentment', and she hits me again: 'Today you choose to be grateful, that's what you do. Being here with these fine friends — you clearly have a lot to be grateful for.' Then she leans in, puts her arm around my shoulder and tells me in a meaningful way that she would be grateful if we paid our bill now before the next shift, so she gets the tips and not the next lady. Who is, apparently, 'a bitch'.

Maybe it was the setting, or the clichéd rom-com nature of the way she delivered her advice, but her words have stuck with me. I often think of that rotund woman, her napkin-based physical assaults and her message of gratitude.

We can always find a way to feel grateful. I could feel resentful because I have to get up early . . . nah, I'll feel grateful I have a job that provides for my family. Resentful that my kids haven't done the dishes . . . nah, grateful that they are healthy and happy. Resentful that my dreams haven't come true exactly as I imagined them . . . nope, grateful for all I have.

Research has shown that a gratitude practice is strongly associated with feelings of purpose in life. It builds relationships, generates positive emotions, helps you enjoy experiences and fosters resilience.

As it turns out, outward-flowing gratitude is even better.

* * *

In a paper called 'Spending money on others promotes happiness', Elizabeth W. Dunn and her fellow researchers show that whether it's nice words, resources, knowledge or cash, giving not only increases happiness for the receiver but also greatly increases happiness for the giver. As the cliché goes, the gift is in the giving.

It might also save your community and the world. In 2010, Adam Grant and Francesca Gino published a paper in the *Journal of Personality and Social Psychology* called 'A little thanks goes a long way: Explaining why gratitude expressions motivate prosocial behavior'. They found that expressions of gratitude sent our way — be they messages, money, gifts, donations or service — make us feel more capable and willing to help others. We also feel more purpose in life.

If you want to make the world a better place for yourself and those around you, you could express gratitude in both words and actual giving. It encourages other people to do the same. Equally, the nastier and greedier your interactions, the worse the world becomes. So send a message telling someone you appreciate them . . . *Boom* — world saved.

* * *

Sometimes your direction and purpose in life is forced upon you. You might get knocked out of aimlessness by tragedy. In hard times, people stand up and gain direction by taking on the challenge in front of them. The obstacle becomes the way. Now you have a path. A sick person to look after, an injustice to fight, a flooded warehouse to drain, a new chef to find, a funeral to organise, a friend to comfort. Whatever happens, you can choose to lean in to what needs to be done and find meaning in that. In this case, the universe has provided you with a direction.

Having said that, the size of the universe raises some questions. In the scale of the universe, our little lives are arguably meaningless no matter what we do. We discussed cosmic insignificance in Chapter Seven, and finitude in Chapter Twelve. At first glance, it would seem that if we are looking to the cosmos for meaning then the numbers are against us. The universe exploded into existence 13.8 billion years ago. Life on Earth began 3.8 billion years ago. Just 150,000 years ago, we started thinking abstractly; language and complex culture began. If the history of the universe was compressed into a single day, modern humans didn't turn up until the last second. We are a speck of a speck in the expanse of time and space; a brief housing of some chemical elements. We mean a lot to our children now, but they will go on without us when we die; sad for a bit, then less so, and not long after that we'll be completely forgotten. Soon after that all humans will be gone, then the Earth, and then the sun.

This sounds bleak, but there is a friendly way to look at the situation. Our small place in time means that *everything matters right now*. Whatever we are made of, and for however long we are around here, we might as well spend our time in the least emotionally punishing way day to day. Our lives are brief, but they're all we have and therefore very meaningful to us. If love and achievement are important to you, then great. If finding some meaning in the life you are living improves the time you have, get on with it. Action is better than inaction. Your chances of being born were one in many hundreds of trillions. You are lucky to exist; you more than likely won't again. So you might as well make something that feels meaningful out of it while you are here.

The Lord of the Rings presents a deep examination of this concept. In my view, the central theme of the epic trilogy is that there is good in the world and it is worth fighting for, no matter the odds nor how briefly we are here.

REAL MEANING

A purpose in life most likely comes from some combination of effort, friction, gratitude, human interaction, love and community. If we are lucky, the fruits of those things can come together all at once in big moments.

A few years ago my second (and equally awesome) son is receiving an award in front of 1000 parents and students at Eden Park's regal Te Pā Grand Hall. We head along as a family and find our seats at the back. He's worked so hard and deserves the recognition, but it's the way he deports himself that hits me in the heart. My little guy standing up in front of so many people with dignity, humour and humility. He slows as he navigates the stairs to the stage, and scans the hall for his family. Then he does something I will remember for a very long time. That perfect little man beams a smile directly at us. He shrugs his shoulders, in a knowing way — 'How crazy is this?' — and then walks confidently to his allocated position by the lectern.

I lose it. Giant lump in the throat; water fills my eyes, hands rise involuntarily to face, bottom lip extends, a small joyous whimper escapes my mouth. Acknowledging his mother, father, brother and grandmother in the crowd is more important to this little human than the award and all the people there.

There is sadness in the moment, too. As he grows, he detaches from us more and more. All the other iterations of his childhood have passed. The little guy in his nappy and cowboy boots; the guy I walked to school on his first day at age five in his massive shorts. All gone. All loved. All missed. Lives intertwined. His time in his mummy's tummy, the drama of his birth (easier than his big brother's, but still so very intense); the hard work of so many of us, including him; the ups and downs, heartbreak, tears, disappointments, injuries, sicknesses, fears, concerns, Christmases, holidays, birthdays, conversations and the jokes that only our family gets all rolled into this moment. Our love, emotional toil and effort manifested in this great little human being — who is now out there on his own, achieving for himself, but still tied to us. It's almost too much to bear. It's pleasure and pain. My heart might explode. To me this is purpose — this is meaning!

Epilogue

The redemption run

A few years after the fateful Queenstown run that I discussed in the preface, the key players are getting back together to do it again. I'm looking forward to a trip away with Scotty, G Lane and Joseph, despite knowing it will really hurt my feet. This time, some of us half-marathon runners will upgrade to a full. I am both terrified and excited about this prospect.

After a few months of build-up, some intense training and a lot of discussion, the big day draws near, and then out of nowhere — it doesn't happen. We all pull out. Not from cowardliness or laziness; the postponement is due to busyness. Everyone is double- or triple-booked. Our professional and personal schedules render the redemption run impossible.

Unperturbed by this setback, we try again six months later, booking an unofficial run rather than waiting for an event. But once again we're thwarted by brutal over-commitment.

Our special run/get-together is proving a challenge to organise, but we are not done yet. Determined to make it happen, we construct a foolproof plan and set a new date. Instead of Queenstown, we will run it in Auckland, where all of us live. With travel out of the picture, a three-day round trip becomes a single-day excursion. Nothing is going to stop us now.

Then — a week before the big day — G Lane pulls a hamstring while skiing and has to be dragged off the mountain on an emergency rescue sledge. While the footage of the incident is highly amusing, the news is also gutting as it means a three-month recovery for him and yet another run date cancelled.

Refusing to give up the dream, we rally together and book in a new date. This time, we all commit to it. We block out our calendars. This run will happen *no matter what.* No excuses. No disasters. Everyone is determined to stay healthy and do it.

But then I don't. The day before, I trip on a tree root during a gentle warm-up run, roll my ankle and smash my head on the pavement. After a trip to A&E, I end up with a set of crutches, a moon boot and a six-week recovery time.

There is no doubt now that we are being tested by the running gods, but we will not go quietly into the night. This positive, life-affirming, health-promoting event *will* happen, even if it kills us. In the face of my injuries, the team regroups and pivots. We band together and, this time, we succeed – the run finally goes ahead.

Well, less of a run and more of a lunch at an Italian restaurant – a stationary run, if you will. The four of us resolve to sit around a table together, go nowhere and feed our faces.

To make this stationary run as authentic as possible, we turn up in our full marathon gear. Shorts, quick-dry singlets, compression socks and hydration packs. It's a huge breach of the restaurant's dress code, but we are here together and that's arguably the main thing.

As the food, drink and conversation flow, we reflect on the past few years. So much has happened since I was sitting on the shores of Lake Wakatipu feeling sorry for myself, thinking about *The Greatest American Hero* and his lost instruction manual.

G Lane has recovered from the rare form of skull cancer that he was diagnosed with. Apart from a scar or two, his head is now close to normal. The skin has grown back across the huge gruesome hole the surgeons had to cut into his face, and he looks great. He still can't move his eyebrows or forehead, and he probably never will again, but apart from a few smallish scars you wouldn't know the horrors the man has been through. Nothing seems to surprise him anymore.

Scotty has been on a journey since he lost his lovely wife, my friend Claire, to a brain tumour — something so tragic for him and their two boys that it's a struggle to comprehend its magnitude. But he has dealt with the whole thing with pure dignity. Scotty always knows the exact right thing to say, which is more than I can say for myself when it comes to Claire's passing. He is an impressive human, the smartest guy you could ever hope to meet, and today he is okay. It's so good to see him laughing and having a good time. Jeez, he looks good.

So does Joseph. Much better than he did when I left him close to death at the finish line four years ago. More on that in a moment.

For my part, back there in Queenstown I was the one with the least problems looming on the horizon, but you wouldn't know it from my sulky behaviour. It took me years of reading, listening and chatting to good people to reach the contentment I feel today.

Back then, in front of that inviting, cold dark water in the middle of the night, I didn't know that I could choose to make things better. I didn't realise that it was me who was making my life more punishing than it needed to be. I didn't fully grasp the power available to all of us when we invite great minds from science and philosophy into our lives. When we take on the ideas of those who, for thousands of years, one after another, have worked on understanding the human condition. There are paths that have been set out — we just have to take the time to become aware of them, then take charge of ourselves and follow them.

Back then, I also doubted the value of exercise, but it's no coincidence that I started my road to feeling better after training for and completing a big run. A bit of fitness can earn you the headspace to entertain making a plan to start feeling better.

This lunch has been dubbed The Seated Redemption Run — but it is only me who has a reason to redeem himself. Four years ago, Joseph was rushed to hospital, having overheated after giving his all to motivate me to make it to the end. 'Come on, Matty; you can do this, Matty; come on, buddy.' The poor guy got me to the finish line, then collapsed. He could have died. I didn't look back, and I didn't check on him. A major medical event was happening to my buddy, and I was munching on bananas and taking selfies a few metres away. Joseph was in big trouble: his heart was beating alarmingly fast; he was critically overheated and had to have all his clothes cut off by emergency staff right there in front of a gathering crowd of onlookers. The first I knew of his plight was his girlfriend calling me to say 'Joseph is in an ambulance, he is not good, he doesn't know where he is — he thinks he's at a cricket match.'

Overheating is unlikely to be a problem sitting around this table today.

But just in case, I will keep an eye out for Joe and make sure he stays well hydrated.

In the hopes of redeeming myself in some small way for that historic finish-line betrayal, as well as the injury that led us here today, I insist on paying for lunch. So we eat and drink and talk about life. Things get deep. It's good.

At the end of 2019, we had no idea of what was to come: personal tragedies, global lockdowns, cancer, natural disasters, shootings, wars, societal division and upheaval. I certainly didn't predict my kids' grandad being hit by a rogue high-speed canoe in his backyard and getting washed away in a violent surge of water. Torrential rain had battered the Auckland region in January 2023, causing severe flooding, and Papa John was knocked over by this unmanned canoe and swept into the creek by his house. From there he was dragged underwater through a storm culvert.

When the phone call came through, we thought we had lost

him. It was grim. I took the car and headed out into the flooding with my son and his mum – Papa's daughter – to see if there was anything we could do to help. If I had been following this unfolding disaster on the news instead of watching a movie I never would have taken our boy, as the car was quickly up to its door handles in the raging rivers that had formed on our suburban streets. Things got scary, but there was no turning back.

Unfortunately our car wasn't seaworthy, and we were never going to get to him in time. While we floated around with a bunch of other vehicles near Auckland's waterfront, Papa John was trapped in what amounted to a concrete coffin. The 75-year-old found himself submerged in water and drifting in and out of consciousness, knowing that if he let go, he could be washed down the next culvert, where certain death awaited.

But Papa John is strong and he was determined to see his family again. He had always loved the water: as a child he collected kaimoana from the seabed, and in adulthood he helped recover bodies as a member of a police diving club. Papa used this training to stay calm, hold on for dear life, and eventually pull his bloodied and broken body out of the drains. Against the odds, and unlike four others across the city that day, he didn't drown; he did, however, suffer terrible injuries, spending a long time recovering in hospital and ending up on the front page of the *New Zealand Herald*. In the accompanying interview, he described what he was thinking while he was underwater: 'This is it. This is how I am going to go out.'

After his long recovery he delivered the following inspirational words.

> I don't blame the water. I am a Pisces man and have been connected to it all my life. I have learned not to sweat the small stuff and just get on with it. I am lucky and grateful to be here and if it was God who saved me then I love him to bits.

A lot of good and bad things happen in this world. Who knows what's coming in the next few days, months or years? What I do know is that here today, I am with good friends, my children are healthy, and we all have roofs over our heads and more than enough food to eat. It would be silly not to enjoy times like these.

It's taken a bit to get to a place where I can appreciate the blessings I have. But the years of own-goals and manufactured problems are over. There are too many real obstacles to deal with to waste our limited time and energy on constructing our own. So, no more ruining the good times by choosing grumpiness, anger and dissatisfaction over gratitude. No more making life more punishing than it needs to be.

Right now, at this second, sitting here with these brilliant guys in this beautiful country — things are pretty good.

That's until the bill comes. Holy shit. Who would have thought that four large men in activewear could consume so much over a mere seven-and-a-half-hour lunch?

The End

References and Further Reading

PREFACE

Henry David Thoreau, *Walden: Or, Life in the Woods*, Thomas Y. Crowell & Co Publishers, New York, 1910.

INTRODUCTION

Marcus Aurelius, *Meditations: A new translation*, trans. Gregory Hay, Random House Publishing Group, New York, 2002.

Ice-T (@icet), 'Highs and Lows . . . After one of the most amazing weeks of my life. I wake up to the news I . . .', 20 February 2023, Instagram (post), <instagram.com/p/Co3BQbkykGd>.

Paul Kalanithi, *When Breath Becomes Air*, Vintage Digital, London, 2016 (Kindle edition).

CHAPTER ONE: ANGRY?

Aristotle, *Aristotle: The complete works*, Pandora's Box, Rainier, Oregon, 2021 (Kindle edition).

Marcus Aurelius, *Meditations: A new translation*, trans. Gregory Hay, Random House Publishing Group, New York, 2002.

JW (@MightBeJohn), 'The hilarious death of the Roman emperor Valentinian the First', Medium.com (website), 30 March 2017, <medium.com/@MightBeJohn/the-hilarious-death-of-the-roman-emperor-valentinian-the-first-f464096bc016>.

Lucius A. Seneca, *On Anger: 'The best remedy for anger is postponement'*, trans. Aubrey Stewart (1889), Montecristo Publishing LLC, 2020.

Dr Joseph Troncale, 'Your lizard brain: The limbic system and brain functioning', Psychology Today (website), 22 April 2014, <psychologytoday.com/nz/blog/where-addiction-meets-your-brain/201404/your-lizard-brain>.

CHAPTER TWO: DISSATISFIED?

Judson Brewer, *The Craving Mind: From cigarettes to smartphones to love — why we get hooked and how we can break bad habits*, Yale University Press, New Haven, 2017.

Marquis de Sade, *Justine, or the Misfortunes of Virtue*, Oxford University Press, Oxford, 2012.

Anna Lembke, in *Dr Anna Lembke — Your Behavior Will Reset 100%*, posted on the YouTube channel 'Neuro Improvement', 22 March 2023, YouTube (video), <youtube.com/watch?v=UwFLTQAQkaU>.

Vipassana Hawai'i, 'R.A.I.N. ~ D.R.O.P.', Vipassana Hawai'i (website), 2 May 2020, <vipassanahawaii.org/resources/raindrop>.

CHAPTER THREE: SCARED?

Karl Albrecht, 'The (only) 5 fears we all share', Psychology Today (website), 22 March 2012, <psychologytoday.com/nz/blog/brainsnacks/201203/the-only-5-fears-we-all-share>.

Nigel Cross, *The Common Writer: Life in nineteenth-century Grub Street*, Cambridge University Press, Cambridge, 1985.

International Shark Attack File, 'The ISAF 2022 shark attack report', compiled by Gavin Naylor, Florida Museum (website), *c*. June 2023, <floridamuseum.ufl.edu/shark-attacks/yearly-worldwide-summary>.

Ethan Kross, *Chatter: The voice in our head (and how to harness it)*, Ebury Digital, London, 2021 (Kindle edition).

David Robson, *The Expectation Effect: How your mindset can transform your life*, Canongate Books, London, 2022.

Lucius A. Seneca, *Moral Letters (Epistulae Morales)*, trans. Brad Inwood & L. P. Gerson, Hackett Publishing Company, Indianapolis, 2017.

CHAPTER FOUR: LONELY?

Catherine E. Amiot & Brock Bastian, 'What is beneficial in our relationships with pets? Exploring the psychological factors involved in human–pet relations and their associations with human wellbeing', *Anthrozoös*, vol. 36, no. 4, 2023, pp. 579–603, <DOI: 10.1080/08927936.2023.2210437>.

Oliver Burkeman, *Four Thousand Weeks: Time management for mortals*, Vintage, London, 2022.

John T. Cacioppo, Stephanie Cacioppo & Dorret I. Boomsma, 'Evolutionary mechanisms for loneliness', *Cognition and Emotion*, 28, no. 1, 2014, 10.1080.02699931.2013.837379.

Alain de Botton, *The Course of Love*, Penguin Random House, London, 2016.

Max Dickins, *Billy No-Mates: How I realised men have a friendship problem*, Canongate Books, London, 2022.

Robert E. Goodin, *On Settling*, Princeton University Press, Princeton, 2012.

Andrew D. Huberman, *Science-based Tools for Increasing Happiness*, Huberman Lab Podcast #98, 15 November 2022, YouTube (video), <youtube.com/watch?v=LTGGyQS1fZE>.

Carl G. Jung, *Memories, Dreams, Reflections*, Vintage Books, New York, 1963.

Matthew D. Lieberman, *Social: Why our brains are wired to connect*, Crown Publishers, New York, 2013.

Vivek H. Murthy, in *Relationships 2.0: An antidote to loneliness* (2020 podcast interview with Shankar Vedantam), Hidden Brain (website), 14 November 2022, <hiddenbrain.org/podcast/relationships-2-0-an-antidote-to-loneliness>.

Vivek H. Murthy, *Together: The healing power of human connection in a sometimes lonely world*, Harper Wave, New York, 2023.

Lauren Powell, et al., 'Companion dog acquisition and mental well-being: A community-based three-arm controlled study', *BMC Public Health*, vol. 19, 2019, 1428, <doi.org/10.1186/s12889-019-7770-5>.

Robert Waldinger, TED talk: *What makes a good life? Lessons from the longest study on happiness*, 26 January 2016, YouTube (video), <youtu.be/8KkKuTCFvzl>.

Mary Williams, 'Exposed: Abandoned in Dunedin's houses of horror', *Otago Daily Times*, 12 August 2023, <odt.co.nz/news/dunedin/exposed-abandoned-dunedin%E2%80%99s-houses-horror>.

CHAPTER FIVE: OFFENDED?

Marcus Aurelius, *Meditations: A new translation*, trans. Gregory Hay, Random House Publishing Group, New York, 2002.

Max Dickins, *Billy No-Mates: How I realised men have a friendship problem*, Canongate Books, London, 2022.

Einzelgänger, *Unoffendable: The art of thriving in a world full of jerks*, published independently, 2019 (Kindle edition).

Janson Media, *The Guinea Pig Club*, posted on the YouTube channel 'Extreme Mysteries', 15 February 2018, YouTube (video), <youtube.com/watch?v=3s3IEX5YrqE>.

David Smith, 'I saw hate in a graveyard — Stephen Fry', *The Guardian*, 5 June 2005, <theguardian.com/uk/2005/jun/05/religion.hayfestival2005>.

Jon Wiederhorn, 'Pages from Kurt Cobain's "journals" published', MTV.com (website), 21 October 2002, <mtv.com/news/9xmuqo/pages-from-kurt-cobains-journals-published>.

CHAPTER SIX: STRESSED?

Amy Arnsten, Carolyn M. Mazure & Rajita Sinha, 'This is your brain in meltdown', *Scientific American*, vol. 306, no. 4, April 2012, pp. 48–53, <DOI: 10.1038/scientificamerican0412-48>.

Nelson Cowan, 'The magical number 4 in short-term memory: A reconsideration of mental storage capacity', *Behavioral and Brain Sciences*, vol. 24, no. 1, February 2001, pp. 87–114, <DOI: 10.1017/s0140525x01003922>.

Nelson Cowan, 'Working memory underpins cognitive development, learning, and education', *Educational Psychology Review*, vol. 26, no. 2, 1 June 2014, pp. 197–223, <DOI: 10.1007/s10648-013-9246-y>.

Yuval Noah Harari, *Sapiens: A brief history of humankind*, Random House, London, 2011.

Sam Harris, *Lying*, Four Elephants Press, Ann Arbor, 2013.

Andrew D. Huberman, *Reduce Anxiety & Stress with the Physiological Sigh*, 8 April 2021, YouTube (video), <youtube.com/watch?v=rBdhqBGqiMc>.

William B. Irvine, *The Stoic Challenge: A philosopher's guide to becoming tougher, calmer, and more resilient*, W. W. Norton & Company, New York, 2019.

William Stanley Jevons, 'The power of numerical discrimination', *Nature*, vol. 3, 1871, pp. 281–282, <doi.org/10.1038/003281a0>.

Brian Krans, 'Nine ways stress is more dangerous than you think', Healthline (website), 4 August 2016, <healthline.com/health-news/mental-eight-ways-stress-harms-your-health-082713>.

CHAPTER SEVEN: HUMILIATED?

Marcus Aurelius, *Meditations: A new translation*, trans. Gregory Hay, Random House Publishing Group, New York, 2002.

Joseph Burgo, *Shame: Free yourself, find joy, and build true self-esteem*, Pan Macmillan Australia, Sydney, 2018.

Oliver Burkeman, *Four Thousand Weeks: Time management for mortals*, Vintage, London, 2022.

Neel Burton, 'The psychology of humiliation: What is humiliation and can it ever be justified?', Psychology Today (website), 27 August 2014 (revised 2 May 2020), <psychologytoday.com/us/blog/hide-and-seek/201408/the-psychology-humiliation>.

Thomas Gilovich, Justin Kruger & Victoria Husted Medvec, 'The spotlight effect revisited: Overestimating the manifest variability of our actions and appearance', *Journal of Experimental Social Psychology*, vol. 38, no. 1, January 2002, pp. 93–99, <DOI: 10.1006/jesp.2001.1490>.

Sam Harris, *The Moral Landscape: How science can determine human values*, Bantam Press, London, 2010.

Rodney J. Korba, 'The rate of inner speech', *Perceptual and Motor*

Skills, vol. 71, no. 3, 1990, pp. 1043–1052, <doi.org/10.2466/pms.1990.71.3.1043>.

Ethan Kross, *Chatter: The voice in our head (and how to harness it)*, Ebury Digital, London, 2021 (Kindle edition).

C.S. Lewis, *Mere Christianity*, William Colllins, London, 2016.

Michael Lewis, *Shame: The exposed self*, Free Press, New York, 1995 (Kindle edition).

Jon Ronson, *So You've Been Publicly Shamed*, Riverhead Books, New York, 2015.

The Tomkins Institute, 'Nine affects, present at birth, combine with life experience to form emotion and personality', Tomkins.org (website), <tomkins.org/what-tomkins-said/introduction/nine-affects-present-at-birth-combine-to-form-emotion-mood-and-personality>.

CHAPTER EIGHT: GREEDY?

P. Brickman & D. Campbell, 'Hedonic relativism and planning the good society', in M. H. Apley (ed.), *Adaptation-Level Theory: A symposium*, Academic Press, New York, 1971, pp. 287–302.

Epictetus, *All the Works of Epictetus: Which are now extant; consisting of his discourses, preserved by Arrian, in four books, the enchiridion, and fragments*, trans. Elizabeth Carter, Hilton Bradley, Dublin, 1759 (reproduction of an original work that is in the public domain).

Amit Kumar, Matthew A. Killingsworth & Thomas Gilovich, 'Spending on doing promotes more moment-to-moment happiness than spending on having', *Journal of Experimental Social Psychology*, vol. 88, May 2020, 103971, <DOI: 10.1016/j.jesp.2020.103971>.

Shaquille O'Neal, in *The Big Emotions with Liz Beecroft*, 29 July 2022, The Big Podcast with Shaq (podcast), posted on the YouTube channel 'NBA on TNT', YouTube (video), <youtu.be/KcTSEcxiXN4>, at 32:35.

Noah Rasheta, *No-Nonsense Buddhism for Beginners: Clear answers to burning questions about core Buddhist teachings*, Althea Press, San Antonio, 2018 (Kindle edition).

Mehrab Reza, 'The basic human desires that drive all purchasing decisions', The Deep (website), 4 April 2022, <thedeep.blog/human-desire>.

Saturday Night Live (TV series), season 44, episode 869, directed by Don Roy King, hosted by Adam Sandler, aired 4 May 2019, NBC, viewed in *Romano Tours — SNL*, posted on the YouTube channel 'Saturday Night Live', 5 May 2019, YouTube (video), <youtube.com/watch?v=TbwIC2B-BIg>, at 1:07.

UT News, 'Spending on experiences versus possessions advances more immediate happiness', UT News (website), 9 March 2020, <news.utexas.edu/2020/03/09/spending-on-experiences-versus-possessions-advances-more-immediate-happiness>.

CHAPTER NINE: ANNOYED?

Marcus Aurelius, *Meditations: A new translation*, trans. Gregory Hay, Random House Publishing Group, New York, 2002.

Alain de Botton, *The Consolations of Philosophy*, Penguin Books, London, 2000.

Derren Brown, *A Book of Secrets: Finding comfort in a complex world*, Transworld, London, 2021 (Kindle edition).

William B. Irvine, *A Guide to the Good Life: The ancient art of stoic joy*, Oxford University Press, New York, 2009.

Paul F. Jennings, 'Report on Resistentialism', *The Spectator*, no. 6252, 23 April 1948, <archive.spectator.co.uk/page/23rd-april-1948/11>.

Robin M. Kowalski, *Complaining, Teasing, and Other Annoying Behaviors*, Yale University Press, New Haven, 2003.

Joe Palca & Flora Lichtman, *Annoying: The science of what bugs us*, Trade Paper Press, 2011 (Kindle edition).

Lucius A. Seneca, *On Anger: 'The best remedy for anger is postponement'*, trans. Aubrey Stewart (1889), Montecristo Publishing LLC, 2020.

Chris Smith interviewing Hugh Hunt in 'The entropy of Christmas lights: Our guests get into a bit of a tangle', The Naked Scientists (website), 21 December 2017, <thenakedscientists.com/articles/interviews/entropy-christmas-lights>.

CHAPTER TEN: BORED?

Sam Harris, *Waking Up: Searching for spirituality without religion*, Penguin Random House, London, 2014.

Mark A. Hawkins, *The Power of Boredom: Why boredom is essential for creating a meaningful life*, Cold Noodle Creative, Vancouver, 2016 (Kindle edition).

Gloria Mark, 'Speaking of Psychology: Why our attention spans are shrinking, with Gloria Mark, PhD', American Psychological Association (website), <www.apa.org/news/podcasts/speaking-of-psychology/attention-spans>.

Shane Parrish, 'Boredom & Impatience' (Brain Food newsletter no. 473), FS (website of Farnam Street Media), 22 May 2022, <fs.blog/brain-food/may-22-2022>.

Dan Shipper, 'How Isaac Newton conquered the loneliness and boredom of quarantine', Every (website), 8 April 2020, <every.to/superorganizers/how-isaac-newton-conquered-the-loneliness-359123>.

Laura Smith, '28 Meditation Statistics: How many people meditate?', The Good Body (website), 19 September 2023, <www.thegoodbody.com/meditation-statistics/>.

Peter Toohey, *Boredom: A lively history*, Yale University Press, New Haven, 2011 (Kindle edition).

Alan Watts, in *Alan Watts on: What's the point of Meditation?*, posted on the YouTube channel 'Road Delta', 5 February 2017, YouTube (video), <youtube.com/watch?v=HoWTbRowoq8>.

CHAPTER ELEVEN: WORRIED?

William R. Beardslee, 'Children's and adolescents' perceptions of the threat of nuclear war: Implications of recent studies', in Institute of Medicine & National Academy of Sciences, eds Fredric Solomon & Robert Q. Marston, *The Medical Implications of Nuclear War*, National Academy Press, Washington D.C., 1986, p. 414, <ncbi.nlm.nih.gov/books/NBK219180>.

Raymond Briggs, *When the Wind Blows*, Hamish Hamilton, London, 1988.

Bill Burr, in *Legendary Comedian Bill Burr — Fear{less} with Tim Ferriss*, 24 June 2022, YouTube (video), <youtu.be/RG0cjYbXxME>, at 54:33.

Leo F. Buscaglia, quoted in 'Leo F. Buscaglia Quotes', Goodreads (website), n.d., <goodreads.com/quotes/229060-worry-never-robs-tomorrow-of-its-sorrow-it-only-saps>.

Dan Carlin, *The End is Always Near: Apocalyptic moments from the Bronze Age collapse to nuclear near misses*, Harper, New York, 2019.

Tim Clare, *Coward: Why we get anxious & what we can do about it*, Canongate Books, Edinburgh, 2022.

Bryan Cranston, *Bryan Cranston's Advice to Aspiring Actors*, posted on the YouTube channel 'Oscars', 28 September 2013, YouTube (video), <youtube.com/watch?v=v1WiCGq-PcY>.

Arash Emamzadeh, 'A new explanation for why some people worry so much', Psychology Today (website), 12 May 2023, <psychologytoday.com/nz/blog/finding-a-new-home/202305/a-new-scientific-explanation-for-why-we-worry>.

Tom Holland & Dominic Sandbrook, *The Fall of the Aztecs* (Parts 1–8), November 2023, The Rest is History (podcast), episodes 384–391, <iheart.com/podcast/867-the-rest-is-history-93597010/episode/384-the-fall-of-the-aztecs-127483585>.

Christopher Kaczor, 'The story of the Chinese farmer', Word on Fire (website), 14 March 2023, <wordonfire.org/articles/fellows/the-story-of-the-chinese-farmer>.

Friedrich Nietzsche and Original Thinkers Institute, *The Complete Works of Nietzsche*, Grapevine India, New Delhi, 2022 (Kindle edition).

Procopius, quoted by Frederick Vervaet in Claudia Hooper, 'Other Awful Years in History', The University of Melbourne (website), 18 September 2020, <https://pursuit.unimelb.edu.au/articles/other-awful-years-in-history>.

David Robson, *The Expectation Effect: How your mindset can transform your life*, Canongate Books, London, 2022.

Dave Roos, 'What is the serenity prayer and who wrote it?', HowStuffWorks (website), 22 March 2021, <people.howstuffworks.com/serenity-prayer.htm>.

Lucius A. Seneca, quoted in 'Stoicism: Letters from a Stoic and the wisdom of Seneca', Academy of Ideas (website), 21 September 2016, <academyofideas.com/2016/09/seneca-letters-from-a-stoic>.

Robert Wright, *Why Buddhism is True: The science and philosophy of meditation and enlightenment*, Simon & Schuster, New York, 2017 (Kindle edition).

CHAPTER TWELVE: GRIEVING?

Marcus Aurelius played by Richard Harris, quoted in 'Gladiator Quotes', IMDb (website), n.d., <imdb.com/title/tt0172495/quotes>.

Oliver Burkeman, *Four Thousand Weeks: Time management for mortals*, Vintage, London, 2022.

William James, *The Varieties of Religious Experience*, Harvard University Press, Cambridge, MA, 1985.

Paul Kalanithi, *When Breath Becomes Air*, Vintage Digital, London, 2016 (Kindle edition).

Ruth Davis Konigsberg, *The Truth About Grief: The myth of its five stages and the new science of loss*, Simon & Schuster, New York, 2011.

C.S. Lewis, *A Grief Observed: A book that questions the nature of grief (Based on a personal journal)*, e-artnow, Prague, 2016 (Kindle edition).

Lucius A. Seneca, *On the Shortness of Life: Life is long if you know how to use it*, trans. C. D. N. Costa, Penguin Books, London, 1997.

John Frederick Wilson, 'What's the point of grief?', The Conversation (website), 13 May 2020, <theconversation.com/whats-the-point-of-grief-137665>.

CHAPTER THIRTEEN: AIMLESS?

Derren Brown, *A Book of Secrets: Finding comfort in a complex world*, Transworld, London, 2021 (Kindle edition).

Oliver Burkeman, *Four Thousand Weeks: Time management for mortals*, Vintage, London, 2022.

Elizabeth W. Dunn, Lara B. Aknin & Michael I. Norton, 'Spending money on others promotes happiness', *Science*, vol. 319, no. 5870, 21 March 2008, pp. 1687–1688 (erratum in *Science*, vol. 324, no. 5931, 29 May 2009, p. 1143), <DOI: 10.1126/science.1150952>.

Scott Galloway, *The Algebra of Happiness: Notes on the pursuit of success, love, and meaning*, Transworld Publishers, London, 2020.

Adam Grant & Francesca Gino, 'A little thanks goes a long way: Explaining why gratitude expressions motivate prosocial behavior', *Journal of Personality and Social Psychology*, vol. 98, no. 6, June 2010, pp. 946–955, <DOI: 10.1037/a0017935>.

Andrew D. Huberman, *Science-based Tools for Increasing Happiness*, Huberman Lab Podcast #98, 15 November 2022, YouTube (video), <youtube.com/watch?v=LTGGyQS1fZE>.

President John F. Kennedy, 'Address at Rice University on the nation's space effort, September 12, 1962', John F. Kennedy Presidential Library and Museum (website), <jfklibrary.org/archives/other-resources/john-f-kennedy-speeches/rice-university-19620912>.

Robert Nozick, *Anarchy, State, and Utopia*, Basic Books, New York, 1974.

Chuck Palahniuk, *Fight Club*, Penguin Random House Australia, Sydney, 1996.

Paul Tsongas, *Heading Home*, Alfred A. Knopf, New York, 1984.

Dan Weijers, 'Nozick's experience machine is dead, long live the experience machine!', *Philosophical Psychology*, vol. 27, no. 4, July 2014, pp. 513–535, <DOI: 10.1080/09515089.2012.757889>.

EPILOGUE

Carolyne Meng-Yee, 'Trapped in "concrete coffin" during Auckland floods: How John Purkis survived after being swept into a culvert', *New Zealand Herald*, 10 March 2023, <nzherald.co.nz/nz/auckland-floods-survivor-john-purkis-was-trapped-in-a-concrete-coffin/SSEYSMO3E5G6JPT7HMRZN3MO2A>.

Acknowledgements

Thanks to my little family of Lani, Charlie and Barry. I love you guys. Sorry if I have been a distracted punisher for the last couple of years while writing this thing.

Cheers to Chris Heath, my amazing dad and the smartest dude I have ever met. Thanks for the advice throughout the writing process and for asking me the simple but very important questions at the start: 'What is your book about? And are you sure you want to write one?' Thanks to Rosemary Heath, the smartest-equal person I have ever met, for being a unique and loving mum, and for thousands of hours of (often heated) philosophical chats. I still miss you every day. Thanks also to my wonderful sisters Imogen, Katharine and Anne-Louise.

Cheers to my buddy Chris Stapp for being the instigator of and my partner in some of the most extreme adventures of my life. You are a talented bastard. Also, thanks for nearly illustrating the cover of this book. Your test drawings were great.

Thanks to Renee Chin for actually drawing the cover, and to Megan van Staden for the design.

Thanks to Michelle Hurley for suggesting I write a book, helping me come up with the concept, then holding my hand through the whole thing. Having never written a book before, I had absolutely no idea what I was doing. Special thanks to managing editor Leanne McGregor and copy editor Teresa McIntyre for all your excellent work on the project. To Mike Wagg and Kate Stone, thanks for proofreading my work; no doubt that was a major operation. Thanks also to Rebecca Simpson, Grace Wang, Krysana Hanley, Nyssa Walsh, Melanie Laville-Moore and everyone else at Allen & Unwin.

Thanks to my uncle Tim Heath for his writing advice and for gifting me his inspirational book, *The Accidental Teacher*. It's a great read — check it out.

To Jeremy Wells, thanks for the tens of thousands of hours of philosophy, science and history chat that we've had while the songs are playing on our radio show. There is nary an idea in this book that I haven't punished Jerry with multiple times.

Thanks to my buddy and the funniest person on earth Phil Brough for being a sounding board throughout this thing. Also thanks to Prong and Spooge. To Cass Donaldson, cheers for being a best bud and for putting up with my punishing book chat over our weekly lunches at the Morningside Tavern. To Phil Smith, cheers for being a great boss back in the day and now a brilliant friend who's willing to listen to my stupid ideas, including many I put in this book.

Cheers to Anastasia Loeffen for giving me great feedback

on the first chapter while we were steamed on a Wellington-to-Auckland flight. I changed direction after that trip. Thanks to Kate Britten for helping me come up with the name of the book — I'm still not sure about it, but thanks. To Mike Sharp, thanks for all the sports, science and philosophy chats over the years. Thanks also for helping me paint my house, and for that time you took me out on your boat into shark-infested waters.

To Tracey Lydiard, sorry about all the things we didn't do because I had to 'write my book'.

Thanks to Chris 'Banger' Goodwin for being a fantastic producer and for teeing up the Zoom interviews when I couldn't work out the time zones. Thanks to Jeremy 'Rooda' Pickford and Finn 'Mash' Caddie for being great mates and for sourcing a bunch of audio and other crap when I needed it for this thing. To Dom Corry, thanks for all the motivational chats on writing and such. To Piers Graham and Gerald 'The General' Stewart, thanks for being good friends and by far the best musicians in our average band Deja Voodoo. Cheers to Brent and Helen Eccles, Maria Robinson and everyone at Eccles Entertainment and Liberation Records, and also to Peter Campbell. My rock 'n' roll adventures that appear in this book are largely thanks to the hard work put in by you guys.

Cheers to Scotty J Stevenson for your fantastic writing advice; I couldn't have gotten this finished without your tips. Also, I never would have started on this in the first place if you hadn't convinced me to take up running.

Tim Batt, you feature in this thing a couple of times. I didn't ask your permission, but you're not the kind of guy who would care about something like that. Also, apologies for shooting you in the neck with a T-shirt cannon. That story was in the book for a while, but I dropped it out of respect for the nearly dead.

Thanks to Adriene Mishler: our hot twenty minutes together every day got me through this process. Bless you and Benji. To Dylan Reeve, thanks for your book-writing advice and app recommendations while we were trapped together on a reality TV show. To Mike Lane, thanks for being a great boss and mate, and for taking me around the world to talk crap about sports. A bunch of stuff that happened on those trips has ended up in this book. A bunch of stuff that happened to your forehead is in here, too, and I appreciate that. (Note to readers: Heath and Lane's 'One and Done MCing' is available for hire for your next event.)

Cheers to Mike McClung, Mike Regal, David Brice, David Ridler, Jason Winstanley, Todd Campbell, Michael Boggs and all the other people at NZME who have given me such an awesome career in radio. And cheers to everyone at Radio Hauraki — Claire, Kate, Prebs, Keyzie, Hoytey J, Minoguey-o, The Notorious Pants Man, The Dark Horse, Gravy, Tom 'Tony' Harper, Pugsley, Jess the Pest, Leigh Hart, Spray It Around Scotty, Matty, Manaia, Ma Clampett and all the rest — you are excellent people. Radio Hauraki is the greatest radio station in the world, and half the stories in this book come from that part of my life. (Readers, you can tune in to *The Matt & Jerry Show* weekdays from 6 to 9 a.m. or listen at your leisure to the highly successful Matt & Jerry Podcast.)

Thanks to Sir Murray Kirkness, Shayne Currie, David Rowe and everyone at the *New Zealand Herald* for giving me a column and for being great people to know, party with and work with. Cheers also to Andrew Stone, Rachel Ward, Anna Harrison, Nick Sorensen and Duncan Gillies for making my punishing weekly columns readable. I would be even worse at writing if it wasn't for you guys. Special thanks to David Rowe for hiring me as Happiness Editor, which led to this whole thing. You are a great dude and an excellent metal guitarist.

Cheers to *The Back of the Y Masterpiece Television* crew, to the *Balls of Steel* (UK) crew, to Stew Williams and Paul and Lee Hupfield, and to Karl Zohrab and the entire team from *The Devil Dared Me To*.

Many thanks to the following brilliant people who agreed to be interviewed by me for this book. I felt totally privileged to talk to Rebekah Ballagh, Max Dickins, Dr Andrea Reinecke, Professor Scott Galloway, Diana Wichtel, Professor William B. Irvine, Oliver Burkeman, Dave Robson, Tim Clare, Ethan Kross, Sam Harris, Tim Finn, Hilary Barry, Andrew Fagan, Dr Anna Lembke, Dr Judson Brewer, Leslie 'The Couch Soiler' Jones (that wasn't me, honest) and Kieran Read.

Cheers to Dave and everyone at the Morningside Tavern, where I interviewed several people for this book and where I punished many more with my ideas over a beer or three.

Thanks to 'Papa John' Purkis for your great stories and writing chat and for your heroic adventure in that culvert, which provided a meaningful end to this thing. Also, thanks for helping me paint my house.

Cheers to Dai Henwood for being my go-to guy for deep Eastern philosophical chat. Thanks also for taking me through your Buddhist tea activities as outlined in the book. To Manaia Stewart, thanks for your words of wisdom. To Jason Hoyte, thanks for being the only other member of the Alternative Commentary Collective elite. It's great to have someone to engage in highbrow philosophical discussion with during a filthy cricket commentary.

Thanks to David Correos, Laura Daniel, Urzila Carlson and Guy Montgomery, the other four members of The Five Friends of Taskmaster NZ Season 2. One of you said something at a lunch we had that I wrote down in my notes and then put in this book. I can't remember which one of you said it, but it was great. I do remember the following advice from Urzila that I used most days on this project: 'If they can do it, I can do it, or it can't be done.'

Cheers to my talent agents at Frank Management: Naomi Ferry and Mike Minogue. Please contact them if you need me for any paid work.

Thanks to Matt 'Mandrake' Perkins and Melissa Robertson for getting me the prison gig. And thanks to Prof Steve Simpson for your political input.

To Joseph Durie, you are a great New Zealander. Thanks for helping source some information here and there, and for not dying when I abandoned you on that Queenstown finish line.

Cheers to my dog, Colin, who has been beside me the whole time I have been writing. Who's a good boy? Colin is! Such a good boy!

Finally, thanks to anyone who buys or reads this book. I really enjoyed writing it — hopefully you get something out of it, too.

Anyway — you seem busy, so I'll let you go.

Bless bless bless.

AUTHOR PHOTO BY MICHAEL CRAIG FOR THE *NEW ZEALAND HERALD*

About the Author

Matt Heath is a well-known broadcaster, producer, actor, podcaster, TV personality and sports commentator. As well as co-hosting *The Matt & Jerry Show* on Radio Hauraki and the Daily Bespoke podcast, he is the co-owner of production company Vinewood Motion Graphics. For ten years he wrote a weekly column for the *New Zealand Herald*. Matt lives in Auckland city and is a father of two.